WHO WILL BE MY TEACHER?

MARTI WATSON GARLETT

WHO WILL BE MY TEACHER?

THE CHRISTIAN WAY TO STRONGER SCHOOLS

WORD BOOKS
PUBLISHER
WACO, TEXAS

A DIVISION OF
WORD, INCORPORATED

Library of Congress Cataloging in Publication Data

Garlett, Marti Watson, 1945–
  Who will be my teacher?

  Bibliography: p.
  1. Education—United States—Aims and objectives.
  2. Christian education—United States. 3. Teacher–student
  relationships—United States. I. Title.
  LA209.2.G37   1985   370'.973   84–29119
  ISBN 0–8499–0471–4

Scripture quotations marked NIV are from
The Holy Bible, New International Version, copyright © 1978
by New York International Bible Society and used by permission
of Zondervan Bible Publishers. Scripture quotations marked TEV
are from the Today's English Version of the New Testament,
copyright © American Bible Society 1976, and used by permission.
Scripture quotations marked RSV are from the Revised Standard
Version of the Bible, copyrighted 1946, 1952, © 1971, 1973 by the
Division of Christian Education of the National Council of the
Churches of Christ in the U.S.A., and used by permission.

Printed in the United States of America

To
my own most significant models, lovers, enablers, prodders,
and interpreters of what is important to know—

my parents, James and Phyllis Watson,
who nurtured me in my beginnings as a learner

and

my children, Marc and Kyle,
who returned me, with their dearness, to the insights of childhood

and, most especially,

my husband, Fred,
who recognized my talents and capabilities long before I did
and who lovingly encouraged my growth toward their fulfillment

CONTENTS

Introduction   11

1. *If I Promise to Be Quiet, Can I Watch What You Do?*
   The Need for Models   17

2. *Will You Still Like Me If I Don't Make Straight A's?*
   The Need for Lovers   42

3. *Do You Know There Are Hurtful Things I Can't Tell You?*
   The Need for Healers   68

4. *How Is It Possible to Learn All This Stuff?*
   The Need for Enablers   92

5. *I Can't Do That—Go Ask Someone Else, O.K.?*
   The Need for Prodders   115

6. *Can You Help Me Understand What's Really Important
   to Know?*
   The Need for Interpreters   144

7. *Do Teachers Really Like to Come to School with Kids?*
   The Need for Learners   172

8. *What Are You Doing the Rest of Your Life?*
   The Need for Commitment   194

Notes   214

Recommended Readings for Further Insights   221

He who knows, and knows that he knows,
   He is wise—follow him.
He who knows, and knows not he knows,
   He is asleep—awake him.
He who knows not, and knows not that he knows not,
   He is a fool—shun him.
He who knows not, and knows he knows not,
   He is a child—teach him.

                —Author unknown—

INTRODUCTION

Where there is much desire to learn,
there of necessity will be much arguing,
much writing, many opinions; for opinion
in good men is but knowledge in the making.

—John Milton—

More and more voices have recently joined in the spirited debate about what is wrong with education and how to make it right. The search for excellence is on. With so much attention focused on such an important and serious issue, momentum now exists for substantial change to take place. Christians can hope that the change will be for the better, or we can do more than hope. We can place ourselves at the forefront of making it happen. In fact, *Christians could be the ones to make the difference between excellence and mediocrity in our nation's schools.*

All schools have tremendous needs. When there is a need, and especially when that need lives among children, the truly vulnerable of our nation, it is not the Christian way to abandon or turn from it. Instead, the Christian way turns toward the need and seeks ways to meet it.

I believe it is implicit in the call of God upon our lives as

Christians to respond in Christ's name. This book will attempt to explain the foundation for my belief and for the specific needs I see Christians able to address in school systems, whether public, private, or even Sunday schools. The authors of *A Nation at Risk*, the report issued by the National Commission on Excellence in Education, wrote: "We wish to note that we refer to public, private, and parochial schools and colleges alike [in this report]. All are valuable national resources."[1]

In this sense we will be addressing a new kind of mission field as we explore what it means to teach Christianly in *all* schools. This perspective is in no way limited to environment. While the classroom education of children traditionally has had little to do with the Christian notion of outreach, we stand to lose much if we do not move beyond that view. Every school in existence needs caring, committed adult participation as never before, adults infused with missionary zeal who are willing to help young people entrapped by "a rising tide of mediocrity."

That phrase, "a rising tide of mediocrity," is the watchword phrase from the National Commission on Excellence report, *A Nation at Risk*, which cast a national spotlight upon schools and the process called education. Far from being the only such report, it was but the forerunner of a whole series of reports that reached similar conclusions about the status of education in the United States.

Close on the heels of *A Nation at Risk* came *Making the Grade*, which called for strong national commitments to excellence in schools. This in turn was followed by the declaration of *Action for Excellence* that "a real emergency is upon us." *Educating Americans for the 21st Century* proposed a plan for improving mathematics, science, and technology education for all elementary and secondary students so that their achievement could be the best in the world by 1995, while at the heart of the "Carnegie Report" (*High School: A Report on Secondary Education in America*) is the conviction that without an improvement in working conditions, efforts to improve teaching are doomed to fail. Finally, with a unique philosophical bent, *The*

Paideia Proposal advocated a broad, liberal, non-vocational curriculum as most appropriate for students in the first twelve grades. All of these reports make valid contributions to our study.

But it is not more proposals that are needed now; it is people. And even more than people, schools need a particular people: they need Christians. A rush to private Christian schooling or, for that matter, to home schooling seems unwise—although I am not precluding such alternatives. There could be some serious dangers waiting for us if these are the main, or only, paths Christians elect to travel. Providing an education based on responsible Christian teaching is not dependent on implementation of politically controversial concepts such as school prayer. To make schools Christian requires a great deal more than allowing prayer or requiring chapel attendance and Bible memory work. In fact, such issues skirt the real needs.

The qualities that characterize an effective school are the same qualities, not coincidentally, that characterize Jesus. And, if we have Christ as our principal, they are within the reach of every school, public as well as private. I am convinced that how Christians respond to the very critical issues confronting the education of *all* our nation's young people will, in the next few years, be the key to success or failure of any changes that are wrought.

The chapters of this book deal with those components that I feel are desperately needed in schools: teachers who model, who love, and who heal deep hurts; teachers who not only enable learning, but even prod and push it into existence; and teachers who will interpret for students what is important to know about life, as well as teachers who are themselves learners. Though each idea is defined and illustrated in a separate chapter, there is nothing independent about what—or Who—unites them. Each attribute is valuable by itself; all together they create responsible teaching. The qualities of good teaching explored here are those I would like to see woven into the fabric of every individual teacher's behavior, with such teachers in front

and at the heart of every classroom. Since it takes real missionary zeal to be optimally effective, we will also be examining how
teachers can overcome those things that cause energy to wither
away. It is unfortunately true that the specter of "burnout"
seeks to engulf good teachers.

Because of their great potential to influence children, most of
this book's focus will be on classroom teachers. More authentically Christian teachers are needed in all types of schools,
teachers who model quiet, not noisy Christianity. As we move
along, we will see that teaching Christianly has nothing to do
with "teaching as preaching."

We will look also at how crucial it is to have more Christian
involvement and participation of every kind in schools. Parents
are needed as partners with the schools in their children's education. In fact, Christian community leaders are needed as partners in this process too, whether they have children in the local
school system or not. These leaders have significant roles to play
in young people's lives. The contribution of such "lay" individuals must be included in our broadening concept of what
teaching actually is.

Let us look hard at Christian investment in public education.
More is at stake for children attending public schools than learning the basics of literacy, vital as that is. If we Christians lessen
our commitment to the public schools by deserting them in huge
numbers, what becomes of the children we don't take with us?
Who is their keeper?

The Gospels tell the story of the children who were brought
to Jesus but were refused access to him by the disciples. The
disciples did not want their Lord bothered with the noise and
commotion of mere children. He was tired, he'd had a hard day,
and he had weighty issues on his mind. In the scheme of things,
how much did these peasant children matter, really?—children
who didn't belong to him, who weren't part of his inner circle?
Jesus didn't have time or energy for them, so his disciples
thought.

Scripture tells us that "when Jesus saw this, he was indignant. He said to them, 'Let the little children come to me, and do not hinder them, for the kingdom of God belongs to such as these'" (Mark 10:14, NIV). And then what did Jesus do? He dynamically underscored his words by taking those children into his arms, placing his hands upon them, and blessing them. Actions, Jesus showed us, count. What we do with our beliefs matters.

In his book *Death at an Early Age,* Jonathan Kozol narrates the disquieting story of eight-year-old Stephen. "Stephen is tiny, desperate, unwell. Sometimes he talks to himself. He moves his mouth as if he were talking. At other times he laughs out loud in class for no apparent reason. He is also an indescribably mild and unmalicious child." Stephen's grades are low, his performance in math and reading already two grade levels below where it should be. He has gone through second and third grades with a string of substitute teachers.

"Nobody has complained about the things that have happened to Stephen," Kozol writes, "because he does not have any mother or father." He is a foster child, trying to survive in the home of people who no longer want him now that he is beyond the cuteness of infancy. "The money that they are given for him to pay his expenses every week does not cover the other kind of expense—the more important kind which is the immense emotional burden that is continually at stake."

With the rejection of Stephen by his foster parents comes physical abuse. Stephen is beaten frequently. He arrives at school with the evidence of the beatings still on his thin, exhausted body. If questioned by anyone, Stephen is "apt to deny it because he does not want us to know first-hand what a miserable time he has. Like many children, and many adults too, Stephen is far more concerned with hiding his abased condition from the view of the world than he is with escaping that condition."[2]

What would Jesus have us do about the Stephens of our world? We are Christ's arms and legs, his eyes and ears. Stephen and his kind need us. And Jesus is depending on us to meet that need. Indeed, he left no question as to what his expectation for us is. "Whoever welcomes one of these little children in my name welcomes me; and whoever welcomes me does not welcome me but the one who sent me" (Mark 9:37, NIV).

There is social dynamite in our nation. Stephen is not a solitary example of the hurt that scars and batters and makes victims of children. There are more incidents of child abuse than ever before, more suicides among children and teens, more drugs and alcohol used as reality-escape valves, an increasing divorce rate, more reconstituted families, and more single-parent families—in fact, more than a third of the white and nearly half of the minority children of this nation live with a mother who provides their only guardianship and who earns less than $10,000 a year.

What would Jesus have us do for these children? Abandon them? See only to the needs of our own children? Who are our "own" children? Christ has said our own children are all children and each is the embodiment of him.

Will that "rising tide of mediocrity" in our country's schools grow to overwhelm us? We didn't ask for it; perhaps we didn't cause it. Obviously it would be less painful to shut our eyes, to inoculate ourselves against the perils assaulting children so that we can go about our daily lives with greater equanimity. But is this the answer, or will we look the problem square in the face? If we do the latter, we will realize that there is a mission field waiting for us in schools—indeed, this particular mission field has desperate need of the special people we can send to it.

CHAPTER ONE

If I Promise to Be Quiet, Can I Watch What You Do?

THE NEED FOR MODELS

Everything the teacher does,
as well as the manner in which he does it,
incites the child to respond in some way or
another, and each response tends to set
the child's attitude in some way or another.

—John Dewey—

Upon receiving her Academy Award for Best Supporting Actress in 1982, Maureen Stapleton gave one of the most memorable acceptance speeches heard at that assembly. Her complete speech went like this: "I'd like to thank everybody I ever met in my entire life."

And she was right. Who could argue with it? Everyone we meet in our lifetime *does* have some type of impact on us. Everyone, in effect, is our teacher. An actress who has mastered the art of utilizing past experience for dramatic characterization, Maureen Stapleton can draw from each encounter with another human being some part of that individual's personality. Later, she taps this reservoir of "quirks" to bring forth yet another brilliant role portrayal. It was that intensive focus on people that allowed the actress in Maureen Stapleton to genuinely "thank everybody I ever met in my entire life." If only each of us could do the same with those whose feet have walked through our lives. Indeed, if only every child grown into maturity could say, "I'd like to thank every *teacher* I ever met in my entire life."

A teacher's impact on a child is a fact. The only variable left in doubt is whether that impact will be for good or for ill. We who work with young people cannot alter whether or not we will have an impact on them. We *will* have one. It is our responsibility to acknowledge the impact and to prepare for harnessing the power we have for good. Christians, in this context, have an important contribution to make to the field of teaching.

Modeling: The Only Way to Truly Teach

"Not many of you should presume to be teachers, my brothers, because you know that we who teach will be judged more strictly" (James 3:1, NIV). A teacher's responsibility may sometimes seem overwhelming. But Christians are prepared to meet that responsibility. "I have more insight than all my teachers," the psalmist said, "for I meditate on your statutes" (Ps. 119:99, NIV). A Christian is in a special position to understand the perspective on people that only God can open up in us. And because this perspective on people is so desperately needed in our schools today, it follows that Christian teachers are desperately needed in our schools too.

It is important, however, that the perspective the Christian brings to the classroom be based on lifestyle and life-attitude, with little or no dependence on direct preaching. Preaching by itself really has very little to do with actual learning. What *does* have to do with learning is the teacher's merging of what is said with what is done—in a word, *modeling*. In public and private teaching situations alike, there is overwhelming evidence that a secure grasp and understanding of the psychological principles of modeling are essential to effective teaching.

I invite you to meet two teachers I know. One is a high school teacher and one an elementary teacher. Both are professing

Christians, and both bring inappropriate perspectives to the classroom in the name of Christ.

Because he was a new Christian, the high school teacher had a genuine and deeply internalized excitement for the Lord. It permeated his whole life, as well it should. After accepting Christ, he looked at his career in a new way. There is nothing wrong with this; such a stance characterizes the main theme of this book. But there was something skewed about the direction he took with it.

In his effort to begin evangelizing non-Christians, the teacher's classroom behavior geared itself toward discovering which students were Christians and which were not. Seen through this filter, everything in his teaching became subordinate to witnessing. He felt an urgency to redeem the lost before it was too late.

Indeed, the more he observed them, the more worried he became about even the professing Christians in his classes. Not unlike teens everywhere who grapple with the inexorable pressures of adolescence, his students behaved with more inconsistency than not. To "help" his students, who worried him constantly, he pointed out whatever seemed inappropriate to him about their behavior or manner of dress. He called them in after class to discuss the tightness of their jeans or sweaters, the shortness of their skirts, the application of their make-up, and where they went on their dates. His admonitions began to carry over into his class sessions as well. He hoped to scare his students into external change with stories of God's vengeance if they didn't do as their teacher recommended—if they didn't mold themselves in their teacher's image, as it were.

I do not doubt his sincerity. He genuinely was afraid his students would be consigned to hell if he did not intervene on their behalf. He believed God had placed him in the school to ensure the "goodness" of his students' behavior and, thereby, to ensure their salvation. Eventually, his desperation to "save" his students took over every aspect of his professional life.

His teaching job was located in a relatively small, deeply religious, mid-American town. Did these demographics, sympathetic as they were to his concern, work in this teacher's favor? No. He was fired before the school year was out. He had lost sight of the importance of modeling and became, instead, embroiled in his own firebrand type of preaching. He talked insistently of God and modeled condemnation and judgment. In the end, it was impossible for anyone in the community to tolerate the teacher's behavior.

The other teacher I want you to meet, the elementary teacher, was not a new Christian. She had grown up in the church, was still very active in church-related affairs, and, when I met her, had been teaching for over twenty years. On the first day of class each fall she was in the habit of announcing to her students that she was a Christian. It was important, she said, for them to know where she stood on that particular issue. Her faith would allow her to do nothing else than be frank and open about her Christian commitment. Throughout the year that followed this initial announcement, she never again mentioned her Christianity. But one thing is certain—her actions were interpreted by others as her definition of Christianity.

So powerful a teaching tool is modeling that by the end of the school year very few of her students wanted to have anything to do with Christianity if what they saw in this teacher was what it did to you. Actually, even the children from strong Christian homes began having their doubts. What was it about this teacher that caused such negative recoil from her professed faith? In truth, she did nothing more than many teachers do.

For one thing, she required everyone in the class to work on the same page at the same time, including those whose ability was well beyond it and those who were beyond being able to comprehend it at all. Without saying a word, she managed to tell her students that they were not individuals to her—that, so far as she could see, there were no differences between them. In a very real sense, she "told" them they were not important as people.

She also created an unnatural environment in which silence reigned supreme. In her classroom there was a firm "no talking" rule. If a student forgot the rule and talked, hundreds of sentences along the lines of "I will not talk ever again" were assigned as homework. Her students learned to hate the act of writing, and worse yet, lost the desire to express themselves on paper, one of the most important and cathartic of human acts.

For any other rule infraction, she upbraided kids verbally. Severe tongue-lashings and public humiliation seemed to be enshrined as deterrents to "crime" in her classroom. She resented support services (such as special reading teachers and gifted facilitators) and often refused to allow the children who were scheduled to see these teachers the flexibility of leaving her room. Perhaps she did not like the implication that she could not adequately meet all the needs of all the children assigned to her. True, she was a Christian, but did she realize that even Christians need help?

If teachers do not model their belief in the innate importance of every child in their classrooms, just the opposite will be communicated. When our nonverbal messages contradict our verbal messages, it is the nonverbal ones that will be believed every time.

Rather than giving us a convenient public platform from which to proclaim our relationship with Jesus in direct, verbal ways, our role in the classroom affords us the opportunity to present *ourselves* as full and real human beings. If we want our students to have the best chance for retaining knowledge and for growing toward maturity, how better can we provide it than through the modeling of being real and being human? What stronger testament can there be to God's wonderful, holistic creation? In this context, teaching is grand witnessing indeed!

Teaching by Showing: Unnoisy Christianity

The "practice what you preach" maxim is not new, of course. It has been around a long time, at least since 1744 when Dr. John Armstrong penned:

Of right and wrong he taught
Truths as refin'd as ever Athens heard;
And (strange to tell!) he practic'd what he preach'd.

Practicing what you believe could be a different, perhaps more relevant maxim for Christian teachers. With this kind of modeling, no preaching need occur. It is "unnoisy" Christianity. Yet observers of it often wonder at its source.

Steve and Bill, two friends of mine, exemplify what I mean. Steve was a professional musician in great demand as a guitar player. For many reasons Steve was in a period of intense anger and rebellion against forces of the world that he felt were out of his control. Bill was in the same profession and knew Steve, though not well. Bill suffered just as many setbacks and disappointments in his career as Steve, yet his philosophical outlook was serene and even, on occasion, outrageously joyous. Unlike Steve, he did not lament his misfortunes. Instead, Bill usually laughed and found something positive and often hilarious about every situation into which his attempts to succeed put him. He was popular with his fellow musicians, all except for Steve. Steve despised Bill.

Steve, in his ever-growing dislike, baited Bill, goading him with sneers and verbal scorn. Steve wanted desperately to penetrate the surface shield surrounding Bill. He was sure an ordinary human being had to be hiding somewhere below the "act." In fact, he became obsessed with uncovering that ordinary human being and revealing Bill for what he was. Steve was right. There was an ordinary human being inside Bill, but Bill never took the bait. Instead, he continued as he always had, being cheerful, being "up," continuing to cope with life's buffets.

Finally, Steve could stand it no longer, and he lashed out in physical anger, actually striking Bill. "I don't know what it is about you!" Steve cried in a rage. Suddenly his own pleading words revealed the reason for the torment he had been feeling: "But whatever it is, Bill, so help me, I want it too!"

Inauspicious as the moment may have seemed, Steve opened himself to learning something of Christ's humanizing love. Bill had not verbalized his relationship with Jesus, the Great Source of his inner peace. Instead of preaching, he had let his quiet modeling serve as his testimony in the tough business of professional music, and it was that which had caught Steve's attention in a way preaching would not have. Bill's modeling spoke louder to Steve than words. After this bellicose beginning, Bill and Steve became steadfast and openly sharing friends.

Unannounced Christianity, or Christian modeling, can be very loud indeed. It can have a lasting impact. When we meet someone who exemplifies a tranquility we don't have, we want it too. When someone demonstrates comfort with his or her own humanness, we long for comfort with ours. Poet Mary Jane Hoberman phrased it accurately: "I know what *I* feel like; I'd like to be *you*."

Children are silent but very watchful observers of what we do. Their wide eyes seem like windows into their souls—and maybe into ours. Truly, children are "God's spies." Coming in innocence and as the "least" of us, children, it could be said, "spy" on what we do. In fact, observing us is the largest part of what children retain about acceptable attitudes and behaviors. Whatever they see us doing, they assume is all right for them too. What they see us do is what they will assimilate as important values for their own lives. "As adults, we are simply unaware of the many, many messages we send," writes Charles Galloway. "And sometimes it's what we don't do that counts the most." Knowing nothing else, we are all entrapped by the limits of our own experiences. We may very well be entrapping our children's futures in the experiences we provide for them now.

"Be careful," we admonish our teenager as he or she leaves the house with the car keys. Yet that same teen has been our passenger for years when we have exceeded the speed limit or crept through stop signs without coming to a complete halt, when we have railed aloud at the antics of a passing motorist

who annoyed us, and when we have maybe even taken un-
justified risks with the entire family's lives in our urge to "get"
someplace. Which message will be retained, the verbal or the
nonverbal?

A professional baseball player caught with cocaine may exclaim to the judge who is passing sentence, "I am not paid to be a
model to kids!" But the teacher does not have that dubious
luxury. Actually, the responsible teacher wouldn't want to
have it (nor should a responsible baseball player). Christ
showed us that the best teaching is modeling. If a teacher cares
about teaching, the teacher understands modeling. There is no
stronger form of teaching. Whether or not it is part of a written
contract with a board of education, the teacher is a model to
kids. Even more, the Christian teacher wants to be a model,
expecting her or his most powerful teachings to come from it.

God: Holy Conjunction Between Words and Deeds

In *Our Children Are Dying,* Nat Hentoff tells of Dr. Elliott
Shapiro, principal of a school in the inner city. While the children of his school can run and laugh and play, Dr. Shapiro sees
beyond their show of external life into inner death. "It's not like
being killed by a car," he says. "There's no blood on them, and
because there is no visible injury, nobody in the middle class is
aghast at the sight. Nobody gets really involved . . . [but] thousands and thousands of children in this city have been dying
because their brain cells have never been fully brought to life."[1]

If even *some* of the children of this nation are "dying," that is
cause for national concern. These children embody the future of
all we hold dear. Every value-rooted ideology is but a short
generation away from extinction. Beyond national concern,
though, must be *Christian* concern, if even some of the children
of this nation are dying. And it is a national shame if Christians
are not concerned.

The verse "Train a child in the way he should go, and when
he is old he will not turn from it" (Prov. 22:6, NIV) is the

Scripture most frequently cited as back-up for whatever edicts we hand down to children. And it is unquestionably a crucial verse for all Christians concerned with the education of children. But the question that must be asked is, What is training?

God provided Jesus as the conjunction between his words (i.e., "I love you") and his deeds (i.e., "Here's my Son to prove it"). Christ, in this context, is the archetype of teaching, the standard, the ideal. Through his Son, God answered the question of what training—or teaching—is: it is modeling. Walt Whitman could very well have been recording this sacred juxtaposition between teaching and learning when, in "Song of Myself," he wrote:

> Behold, I do not give lectures or a little charity,
> When I give I give myself.

Because he gave himself fully for God's instructional purposes, Jesus underscored all that he said, making his words one long italicized proclamation. It is unlikely we would marvel at his words if he had not so perfectly used his actions as convincement. What captivates our attention is the fact that he did not so much talk about an amazing life as live one. Taking ordinary people as his closest friends, going to the homes of despised people and eating with them, dying on a cross like a common thief when he literally had all the power in the world to save himself—these are the actions from Christ's life that make us sit up and take notice. When our interest is caught, our introspections begin, and then—and only then—are we able to truly learn. Jesus *showed* us what he wanted us to internalize, what we need to believe and comprehend if we are to become fully alive and authentically human. Through Christ's astonishing messages in motion we are enabled to learn.

Paul understood how "seeing is believing" works. As Christ taught him by example, so Paul taught others. "My message and my preaching were not with wise and persuasive words, but with a demonstration of the Spirit's power" (1 Cor. 2:4, NIV).

Words alone were not the persuasive part of Paul's ministry; they became so only when coupled with actions.

The principle applies to contemporary classrooms too. A teacher is giving instructions to the class for a future assign' ment. One boy in the class has either failed to listen attentively or failed to understand. At any rate, the boy holds up his hand and asks a question about the assignment being given. The teacher stops in mid-explanation, looks momentarily disgusted at the interruption, and says pointedly, "I just finished explain' ing that. Where were you?" Embarrassed by the reprimand, the boy pursues his confusion no further. Later, while talking to a parent within this same student's hearing, the teacher says, "I always tell my students the only stupid question is the one that's not asked."

Which message is believed? The one that is spoken, or the one that is modeled? The answer is obvious. True, modeling de' pends upon words to solidify its point. But Jesus did not rely solely on words. He linked those words with dynamic, startling actions. That way, his words became indelibly etched into the minds and hearts of mankind for eternity. He was, and is, the perfect teacher.

Jesus: Our Model for Modeling

Jesus' form of teaching was most dynamically demonstrated in his modeling. While he gave us the new commandment to love one another, he went one step further than just saying the words to us. And it was that step that has had its lasting impact on us as his "students." He showed us how to love others by loving others. Modeling was his teaching technique. It is as simple as that: Jesus revealed that learning occurs when model' ing is done.

Saying "it is as simple as that" does not mean that it is easy. It is not. But apart from its difficulties, working with people is fascinating. It cannot be dull when personalities are so different. Still, the "interest" aspect of teaching intermingles with the "difficult" aspect and provides the puzzling challenge: how to deal effectively with all those unique personalities at the same time. It will be helpful to look at the qualities Jesus modeled and discover something of how he did it. As David McKenna writes in *The Jesus Model,* "If Jesus developed the stature of a whole and effective human being, he . . . becomes a 'significant other' and deserves a following."2

When we examine his life as a human being, the first characteristic we see is Jesus' spontaneity. He was not tied to traditional ways of doing things. He was not concerned with impressing others. He washed the disciples' feet instead of having them wash his, even though he was their master. He struck up a forbidden conversation with a Samaritan woman at a well. His close friendships included several women, a shocking defiance of the conventions of his day. He had the ability to be spontaneous and at ease in a variety of situations.

A second characteristic is Jesus' respect for diversity. He demonstrated freedom from prejudice and jealousy. He surrounded himself with all manner of people—respectable women, "fallen" women, lepers, detested tax collectors, rich men, poor men, working men, indigent men. He befriended Jews and Gentiles alike, no matter their class, no matter their background. He looked down on no one, even to the point of dying on a cross as a common criminal so that there was literally nobody left in the world whom he could look down upon, even if he had wanted to. By being "better" than no one, he modeled acceptance of us all.

Third, we can see Christ's sense of humor and his ability to enjoy himself. His parables contained humorous illustrations: a camel going through the eye of a needle, tax collectors getting into heaven ahead of priests. "By laughing at the pretense of humanity," McKenna writes, "he was laughing at himself."3 Jesus was a very social man who enjoyed being in the company of people so much throughout his life that his enemies accused him of being a drunkard and a glutton (Matt. 11:19). Until Jesus changed the image, the pattern of social denial chosen by John the Baptist had been the standard by which religious devotion was judged.

Yet, through a fourth characteristic, we discover Jesus' recognition of the need for privacy, for solitude, for opportunities to be by himself and see his life from a contemplative perspective. This, too, must be a model for full humanness since it was important to Christ. The Gospel of Mark, for example, records twelve separate times when Jesus chose to get away by himself. Anne Morrow Lindbergh said of solitude that "there is a quality to being alone that is incredibly precious. Life rushes back into the void, richer, more vivid, fuller than before . . . you are whole again, complete and round—more whole, even, than before, when other people had pieces of you."[4] Jesus modeled what she was talking about.

Jesus was creative. His inventiveness is a fifth characteristic. Nearly everything he did spoke to his fascinating aptitude for coming up with new ways of doing things. Why press grapes when water can become wine? Why pack sack lunches when two fish and five loaves will feed thousands? Why live like a rich ruler when there is simple joy in planing wood in a carpenter's shop? Why *tell* people who you are when you can let them *see* it? There is no doubt that Jesus' imagination was active and delightful. Scripture is replete with accounts of it.

Despite Jesus' creative approach to problem solving, he respected life's complexities and did not intimate there are simple solutions to difficult questions. This is a sixth characteristic he modeled throughout his life. There are no neat categories for fitting things into. Life is not a matter of following a set of prescribed rules—this makes you right, that makes you wrong. Peter, a beloved disciple, crumpled under stress and denied he even knew Jesus, much less that they were friends. Peter, the Rock, was weak and faithless Yet Jesus reinstated Peter. It was not a situation which could be viewed in simple black and white terms: now you're good, now you're bad. The parables Jesus told further emphasized his profound understanding of the complexities of human behavior.

The parables illustrate a seventh fascinating aspect of Jesus' human character too; he was a marvelous storyteller. His goal for us was to learn from the stories, of course, but that did not lessen his enjoyment in their telling. He seemed to delight in the act of teaching as much as he looked forward to its outcome.

By focusing on Christ when we work with children, we can utilize the resources of our "principal." He is the backbone, the giver of energy and sustainer of commitment, the role model for role modeling. In fact, the positive role modeling educators bring to their task is a direct gift from God. They owe that ability to no one but God. Jesus acknowledged who it was who gave him his abilities. It was God. God provides this special perspective on people, and Christ demonstrates how to use it.

Tangible Wisdom: The Modeling of Human Teachers

We have looked at seven important qualities of Jesus that serve as our model for modeling. Understanding and knowing these qualities is important; it is equally important to see how they can stretch into actual school settings where they will do good and contribute to students' lives.

I want to share with you some vignettes of a few very fine classroom teachers I know. These men and women already rec' ognize this fresh way of looking at themselves in the perfor' mance of their jobs. In varying ways, they demonstrate the reality of Jesus. In them is found human wisdom, and it is their perspective that is needed in the "mission field" of teaching.

Jesus modeled spontaneity. Nick, a teacher who feels free to think and act spontaneously, has a fourth grade class. His room has been caught in the ravages of a long, bleak January. Outside the window is nothing green, nothing clean. Nick has planned classroom activities that are not based on the time of the year. This is not primarily to keep minds off cheerless winter days, though he appreciates that side effect.

Suddenly the clouds crack a bit and the first snow of winter begins to fall. Huge flakes drift down, blanketing the brown spaces beyond the window with cold, white beauty. Nick's students respond with murmurs of relief; their pent-up expectation can at last be released. They knew it would happen sooner or later, but the suspense is finally over. Nick shares their excitement, and closing up his carefully structured plans for the afternoon, announces, "Everyone get your coats and hats on. We're going for a walk in the snow."

Nick is a teacher who is not rigid, who is flexible, and who loves spontaneity as much as his students. Because of it, he is modeling part of what it takes to be fully human.

Jesus modeled an appreciation for diversity. Barbara, a good friend of mine and an excellent teacher, recently received a grant to install a conference-style WATS telephone in her social studies classroom. Through this hook-up, she and her students can now call anywhere in the United States and at least one place abroad. They begin their year by planning who they want to call. Should it be congressmen, Supreme Court justices, movie stars, corporate executives, professional athletes, the pope, England's prime minister? They draw up a list of specific names and send out letters, requesting an appointment time when they can call and conduct a telephone interview. Several favorable responses come back from intrigued national, and even some world, leaders. Finally, telephone interviews are arranged, and the calls from the classroom begin.

These are exciting and memorable moments for the students and their teacher. By helping develop a strong sense of unity and brotherhood among all human beings, no matter how diverse, Barbara increases the realization of what it takes to be fully human.

Jesus modeled a sense of humor. Mavis, a high school English teacher, is a rather sophisticated woman, well-groomed, nicely dressed, but a stern taskmaster, a thoroughly no-nonsense teacher. Still, she is popular with her students.

Cut-Off Day is an important spring ritual at the school where Mavis teaches. On Cut-Off Day the kids pile into the building wearing all types of cut-off pants and shorts and assorted old clothes. A festive atmosphere clings to the classrooms. None of the kids really expect cultured Mavis to be in cut-offs, and when they get to her room, they see they're right. Mavis is in her usual neat dress. As her students enter the room, Mavis jokes about their attire, but when the bell signals time to begin class, she becomes brisk and teacher-competent again.

She teaches as she always has, writing across the chalkboard, filling their minds, as they fill their spiral notebooks, with her words. About halfway through the period she suddenly stops talking, turns to face her class, and then, as if startled into remembering something she had all but forgotten, she pulls up her dress, exposing a pair of extremely faded, old blue-jean cut-offs. The class goes wild, hooting and whistling, stamping and applauding. Carefully and deliberately, with a show of genteel fastidiousness, Mavis lets her skirt fall back into place. Then she resumes her teaching.

Mavis has a sense of humor that is appreciatively acknowledged by her students; indeed, they need to see their teacher demonstrate it. The ability to laugh at ourselves, and to invite others to laugh with us, is an important part of what it takes to be completely human. And we learn it by having it modeled to us.

Jesus modeled the benefits of solitude. Joan teaches first grade and knows the therapeutic value of time spent alone. She has designed a hefty contraption which her willing husband, Tim, has helped her build. When it's finished, it is sturdy, though not necessarily a thing of beauty. Still, it creates quite a stir among the children on Monday morning. "What is it?" they want to know. "Can I go up in it? By myself?" And Joan smiles and nods and tells them the rules for use of the "tree house," as it will come to be known.

Certainly not an antisocial individual, as her co-workers can attest, Joan nevertheless values her moments of privacy and solitude. She knows her students, children though they are, will value time to themselves too. Her lack of need to exhibit control over their lives allows Joan to give her students the gift of an occasional "time out," an opportunity to get off by themselves now and again and contemplate the world from a different perspective. Joan is modeling an understanding of solitude, an important requirement for *staying* human.

Jesus modeled joy in creativity. Philip is a highly imaginative person. The desks in Philip's classroom used to be rigid, each seat attached to each desk by a heavy metal rod. They were old-fashioned desks, designed for use in rows. They still had the holes in the tops where inkwells once stood. Ready for the trash heap, they were, at long last, destined to be replaced by newer, more flexible modular furnishings.

Philip asked Ruth, the principal, if he could do whatever he wanted with the desks, since they were going to be discarded anyway at the end of the year. Knowing Philip's inventiveness, Ruth regarded him curiously but answered, "Sure, why not?" So Philip, artist that he is, asked his students to think of what they would like a picture of. It needs to be a picture they want to keep, he tells them, something they would like to look at every day. He'll draw part of it, and they'll draw part of it. As the class plans its pictures with Philip, he begins to draw right on their desktops. Amazing! They've never seen a *teacher* doodle on desks before. But whatever they tell him they want—an elephant on a bicycle, a rocket ship, a house with flowers around it—Philip draws it with big, bold sweeps right on their desks. And then he hands each student the drawing pencil for them to finish the details. In another week the class will have their desktops painted and enameled, and that is where each child will do schoolwork all year.

Philip's room is alive with color and individuality. When May comes, Philip removes the desktops and sends each child home with a hand-painted remembrance of the year. (David, a college student of mine, was in Philip's classroom and still has his desktop.) Because Philip sees everyday life as being filled with possibilities for creativity, because his inventive mind is never at rest, he models one of the things it takes to be fully human.

Jesus modeled a respect for complexity. Harvey, a junior high coach, knows that life does not offer easy answers to difficult questions. He is aware that there is no ready-made formula to follow for dealing with his students. One day during football practice a fight erupts between Jeff and Mitch. They each accuse the other of starting it. It is a physical, name-calling disagreement. Harvey, calm and soothing, separates the boys. He listens patiently to Jeff's version and to Mitch's. He asks clarifying questions, demonstrating to each boy that he has heard their differing viewpoints.

Then Harvey poses another question. "Is only one of you right and one of you wrong?" he asks. "Or can you both be right about some of it, and both be wrong about some of it?"

The three of them talk through the event again, searching for places where each may have had a valid complaint and where each may have been "out of line." Harvey does not force either student into a win/lose situation. Life is not like that. Because Harvey is careful not to shape or mold reality into neat categories but, rather, accepts it with all its complexities, he is demonstrating one of the important characteristics it takes to be fully human.

Jesus modeled a delight in the act of teaching. Recently I was reading E. B. White's famous description of the barn from *Charlotte's Web* to my college students. I love that book. White's prose evokes sensory images and authentic emotions. "Listen to that!" I will invariably exclaim when I read it. "Can't you just see that barn? Can't you just smell it?" It never ceases to amaze me that one human being can write for another human being in vocabulary so rich and with images so powerful that words and pictures all but leap from their pages. Having received a first edition of *Charlotte's Web* from my grandparents when I was a young child, and having taught for a number of years, this was by no means the first time I had read the book. It may not have been the fifty-first either. Actually, I have lost count. But White's eternal story always stirs me, always sends my imagination onto an empathic journey.

Life can be extraordinary in its very "ordinariness." Through reading and re-reading marvelous children's books, I can find renewed pleasure in living. I expect that, if you are like me, you know what I mean. But if children's books aren't as important in your life as they are in mine, perhaps you experience what I'm talking about with springtime and rainbows, with the texture of corduroy and the weave of wool, or with any of the other sensory joys available to us in the physical world.

If we share our honest enthusiasms with those close to us, we can model excitement for the simple delights of living. And, as Christ did, we can enjoy the act of communication with others—indeed, of teaching. I hope that my reading aloud will cause my students in turn to read aloud to the children in their classrooms. But even if my students never pass on this particular love, together we have experienced something memorable.

Models of full and rich humanity are alive and well in some school classrooms and could be alive and well in all of them. The number of things a teacher can do are limited only by his or her spontaneity, respect for diversity and individuality, sense of humor, creativity, appreciation for complexity, and ability to be a quite ordinary human being.

Mental Health: Models for Attaining Wellness

Jesus was a fully human man. He was, in Abraham Maslow's terms, *self-actualized.* In his classic study, *Toward a Psychology of Being,*[5] Maslow describes the process of self-actualization as "becoming the self that one truly is." In order for self-actualization to occur, Maslow postulates a developmental sequence in which basic needs that we all have must be met. First come physiological and safety needs, then love and belonging needs, followed by esteem needs, knowledge and understanding needs, and aesthetic needs. After this process occurs, according to Maslow, we are ready to move on to self-actualization, that is, to respond to the pull on us to grow toward our human potential.

Said another way, if we are each to become fully human, like Christ, we must find some means of meeting our needs to be comfortable and to be safe, to love and be loved, to be worthy of respect, and some means of having our questions answered as well as having opportunities to experience beauty. Every human being has these needs; if any need is left unmet, the ability to realize full human potential is unlikely. You cannot, obviously, appreciate a fine piece of music (aesthetic need) if you are cold and hungry (physiological need). Implications for what a classroom should become abound from Maslow's study. Every child, every student, every human could be positively affected by his important findings.

But in his studies of psychological well-being, Maslow arrived at the conclusion that the characteristics of self-actualization he found in older adults did not exist in developing young people. He surmised that societal factors kept young people from achieving their potential at an early age and that the best we can expect and hope for them is a "growing well" situation in which we see them striving to make full use of their talents and capacities. Young people moving toward becoming all that they could be are those who are doing what they are capable of doing.

The question begs for an answer: Are schools providing opportunities for students to do what they are capable of doing? Are we, in fact, moving young lives down the road toward attainment of their potential, toward becoming fully and wonderfully human? Are we *modeling* qualities of humanity?

Maslow discovered fifteen characteristics common in those individuals who are self-actualized. He intended, by defining them, for these characteristics to provide a composite picture of a well-adjusted individual that could serve as a goal (or as a role model) for all of us. Here is where "growing well" begins taking on dynamic properties for those of us concerned with education. There will only be a "growing well" situation in schools when

there are teachers and other adult care-givers who provide living examples of what it is to *be* fully human.

The people who can make a real difference in teaching today
are those who understand complexity and do not mold reality
into neat categories. These are people who accept themselves,
who have nothing to hide, and therefore, nothing to protect.
These are people who are spontaneous, who delight in the ordinary, and who with good humor tend not to take themselves too
seriously. These are people who are relatively free from prejudice and jealousy. They are builders of bridges to others, forming
deep and rich relationships with both men and women. They
recognize the need for contemplation, for moments of solitude
and privacy. They are as interested in means as they are in ends,
they enjoy the work involved in achieving a goal as much as the
goal itself, and they are creative and inventive in their everyday
lives. They are people who respect diversity and individuality.

What is needed in schools today are people who not only
think it's all right to be human, they think it's the only thing *to
be*. We have already seen that, not surprisingly, these characteristics are the very same ones Jesus exemplifies. This is why I
believe so strongly that Christians and not more proposals can
bring about real educational excellence. If we who work with
children can ourselves be these fully human people, we can
model what it is to be human. "A young child has very little
capacity for abstraction and symbolic meanings," writes Raymond Cramer in *The Psychology of Jesus and Mental Health*.
"He takes things at their face value."[6] In other words, children
are concrete thinkers. They need to see and touch and grab hold
of what we want them to learn. They will "take in" exactly
what we "give out." What children are, we have taught them
to be.

In our modeling of the humanity of Christ is a vision for
attaining wellness for all. Because we can visualize our students
being well through Christ, and because we know that attaining
self-actualization is in God's plan for every person, modeling can
become part of true Christian commitment, part of a dynamic

conceptual framework leading toward real and meaningful teacher action. It can make school classrooms a whole new, exciting mission field.

Teaching without Classrooms: Modeling for All

We have been focusing our attention on teachers and class-rooms. But each of us whose life intersects with a child's life has the potential to have an impact on that child. Parents certainly are models. But so are aunts and uncles, grandparents, busi-nessmen and women and other community leaders, neighbors, clerks in stores, passing motorists, church acquaintances—all have responsibilities for helping nurture full and glorious hu-manness in children.

The list of those who could contribute to this goal is endless because there is virtually no one who does not occasionally cross paths with a young person. Each of us could be a model. In fact, even without our being aware of it, each of us already *is* a model. We are observed at whatever we're doing. Here, then, are a few practical ways we can each function as a positive model to children, no matter what our jobs.

We can model an appreciation for reading as recreation. If we are concerned about illiteracy in this country—or even al-iteracy (a new class of people who can read but don't)—then one of the best things we can do is show a love for books and reading. Subscribe to a newspaper and selected magazines, and be seen reading them. Give books as gifts to children you know. Haunt garage sales for literary treasures that you can give away (I once bought C. S. Lewis's entire *Chronicles of Narnia* for thirty-five cents!). Take out a library card with a young person. Offer to run a neighborhood "shuttle bus" to the library for storytimes and puppet shows. In a word, *model* the importance that you say you attach to reading activities.

And if you have children in your home, read aloud to them *every day*. Research shows there is nothing more important you can do to foster a lifelong love affair with reading. Don't wait to start until they can talk, and don't stop just because they get old enough to read for themselves! Whenever you travel in the car, on vacation trips or other long outings, read aloud to the whole family as you go. It will break the monotony of seemingly end-less drives and kindle an appreciation in even the adult members of the family for books and for reading. Be sure to obtain a guide to good read-alouds. There are several such guides on the mar-ket. The world of children's literature is a wonderful adventure that Christian families need to be exploring together.

Another important quality that children must pick up from someone, if they are to remain mentally healthy, is that of being able to admit mistakes and apologize for them. Somehow many of us feel it will cripple our authority with children if we admit that we "blew it." Yet we all occasionally blow it. We do things that get misinterpreted, we say things we didn't mean to say, we are unnecessarily harsh, we behave and speak thoughtlessly and unbecomingly.

If we never model the simple act of saying "I'm sorry," we imply that we are never wrong, that we are somehow more perfect than children are. If there is tension between us and a child, and we do not verbally accept any responsibility for our contribution to the tension, we have so much as said that we are blameless. And if we have no blame at such times, by implica-tion children have all of it. We could be sending them toward adulthood with heavy amounts of assumed guilt. They could very well develop insecurities about their worth and abilities as they grow up. They could learn to conceal the truth, to lie, in an effort to thwart discovery of their imagined imperfections. They will decide they are bad, and if found out, will no longer be able to keep the love of those important to them. Their only hope is that no one will ever realize how awful they really are.

But if young people see and hear adults apologizing and mak-ing sincere confessions of wrongdoing, they are more likely to accept the idea that all people make mistakes. Let's get about the business of admitting our own failings in order for this insight to develop in children. Self-disclosure is possible for each of us. It needn't be just a child we apologize to; we can and should offer a genuine apology to anyone we have wronged. If a young person overhears the acknowledgment of error, a healthy impact is made—though this should not be our motivation for expressing sincere regret. Unfortunately, I know some children who have never been personally apologized to. This is appallingly destruc tive to their capability for becoming fully human.

Jesus modeled still another quality that we too can, and must, model: the quality of forgiveness and of reacceptance into the fold. Remember the example of Peter denying Christ and of Christ reinstating Peter after this grievous act. Young people will err; they will tax our patience; they will disappoint us. But punishment that presents a stumbling block to developing a healthy self-concept is a lifelong punishment, and such punish ment is not at all what Jesus demonstrated as a response to mistakes, no matter how foolish. In Christ's view, there is no such thing as irreparable damage. How can we imply otherwise? Indeed, Peter provides us an exemplar for how loving forgive ness can help a person's sincere effort to become a completed human. When presented with Christ's love, weak Peter grew strong.

A fourth mode of positive modeling is to show respect for children's personhood by giving them the dignified attention they deserve. Nothing is more demeaning for a child than to stand at a theater concession stand and be continually passed over because bigger, more aggressive people make their wants and needs known first. My own children, during their younger days, felt rejected as important human beings when servers overlooked them in this way. Yet they were short enough that it was relatively easy to do. Perhaps those in service jobs, like waiters and waitresses and clerks at counters, could glance downward more often and see who is there looking up at them.

This is true in a church too, even though we might be reluc tant to admit it. We tell children we want them involved in church. We even give them gifts of Bibles at various milestones along the way. But what we frequently do not give them is a bulletin during Sunday morning worship services. Ushers will dispense bulletins to the adults in the family as they enter the sanctuary but often not to that family's youngest members. Whether they can read it or not, by not even giving them a bulletin we communicate to children that they are of lesser importance. Sometimes we don't look at them either, as if our eyes cannot quite see that low, and often we don't greet them.

My husband directs the choir at our church and I sing in it, so our youngest son, Kyle, often sits alone on Sunday morning. Frequently during our programmed greeting time I see Kyle standing by his pew, ignored by the adults milling noisily around him. I have even seen him put his hand out when he thought someone was heading his way, and then, discovering his error, react by thrusting it quickly back at his side. But when a thoughtful adult goes out of his or her way to shake Kyle's hand and wish him a good morning, his face reflects his gratitude at being acknowledged.

Surely the cruelest punishment that could be devised for any of us would be to send us into the world to be absolutely ignored by everyone we encountered along the way. Personhood does not begin at age eighteen or twenty-one, and the stimulation of healthy self-worth cannot wait until then. It must begin with infancy and carry on from there.

Through "copying" what their teachers do, students can learn courtesy, courage, honesty, honor, sportsmanship, kindness, and unselfishness. Or, through copying, students can learn exactly the opposite. What this really means is that we have the potential to teach students how to be fully and wonderfully human simply by providing an example of it.

In the classic A. A. Milne children's stories and verses, Christopher Robin is a companion Winnie-the-Pooh looks up to and emulates in all things. Milne records Christopher Robin's contemplation of the profound impact he has on Pooh.

> Wherever I am, there's always Pooh,
> There's always Pooh and me,

Whatever I do, he wants to do:
"Where are you going today?" says Pooh;
"Well, that's very odd 'cos I was too.
Let's go together," says Pooh, says he.
"Let's go together," says Pooh.

I once stood on the sidelines at a mixed-league softball game in which some friends of mine were playing. At game's end, one of the teams was vociferously taking issue with an umpiring call that disallowed a run they believed should have counted. Verbal abuse spewed into the air. It continued for several long, loud minutes. Casting my eyes down a bit (I was rather embarrassed to look at the scene directly), I had a worse shock.

There, in the middle of this adult foray, stood a little girl about four years old, striking her small balled fists against the umpire's leg, yelling, "We got that run! We got that run!" She seemed unnoticed by all except the umpire and myself. Finally, the umpire abruptly turned and left, signaling the argument's end. Apparently believing she had scored some sort of moral victory by pitching in and "helping" foment this climate of bitter challenge, that angry child then folded her arms across her chest and flounced, chin up, back to the bench with her adult role models. Children, whether we hear them or not, are suggesting, "Let's go together." And so, whether we pay attention or not, they are.

CHAPTER TWO

Will You Still Like Me
If I Don't Make Straight A's?

THE NEED FOR LOVERS

Wilbur blushed. "But I'm not terrific, Charlotte.
I'm just about average for a pig."
"You're terrific as far as *I'm* concerned,"
replied Charlotte, sweetly, "and that's what
counts. . . . I think you're sensational."

—E. B. White—

There was once a mother who loved her son very, very much. She knew him well, and she knew when he suffered. One of the things that caused him to suffer was change. He liked stability in his relationships and did not take well to change. She had seen this happen many times.

When he was two, the family made its first move. It was a geographic move which took the boy several hundred miles from the home where he had been born. No one expected a two-year-old to even notice the change. But he did. He never talked about it—at two, how could he articulate it?—but his consternation expressed itself through illness. He spent his entire second birthday, which was celebrated the day of his arrival in his new home, with continuous bouts of vomiting. Presents, cake, enticements in his honor held no interest for him. Moving had made him physically ill.

42

At age four, he moved with his family again. He followed his mother around through their new house while she unpacked and fretted over boxes. He never once let her out of his sight, perhaps fearful that she would disappear as unexpectedly as his familiar surroundings had. His blanket did not leave his hands either. Indeed, after this move, he slept with that blanket until well into middle childhood.

Another two years passed and once more the family moved. The boy began school in his new environment, but he wanted to keep calling his friend on the phone, his friend back in the old neighborhood. It was a long distance call, and he wasn't allowed to place more than one or two of them. So he kept his friend's picture near his bed where he could see it every day.

The family did not move again until the boy was beginning fifth grade, and this time the move was only a few blocks away instead of hundreds of miles. He did change elementary schools, but his old friends were well within easy bike-riding distance. His mother thought this would help, yet still she saw her son brooding, keeping to himself throughout the settling-in time in his new home.

When school began again and he took off for his first day of class, she watched him worriedly. She made arrangements to be home at lunchtime so he would have a break in his day which encompassed familiarity: her. He came home, and she asked him with some trepidation about his new school.

Oh, he hated it, he said. It was terrible.

Why, she asked, stalling for time as she tried to strategize how best to help him deal with this situation.

Because no one played with him, he said. At recess, nobody paid any attention to him. They all had their own friends, they knew each other already. He didn't fit in. School *could* be okay, he allowed in fairness, but recess was going to ruin its chances.

Well, she told him, she was sure it would get better. After all, it had only been one morning. Give it time, she urged as she sent him back to school for the afternoon.

After school, even though she was a working mother, she was

home once more when he got there, waiting at the door with a smile of encouragement. She didn't want him coming home to an empty house. Not yet.

"Better?" she asked brightly, fully expecting a miracle to be impossible but wishing fervently that it wasn't.

He grinned at her. "Yes!" he said. "*Much* better!"

She didn't want to let on that his answer surprised her, but it did. In fact, it astonished her. "Why?" she asked. "What was different about the afternoon? Did the kids play with you? Are they starting to get to know you?"

"No," he said.

She looked at him, puzzled. "Well, then, what?"

He shrugged, rummaging in the refrigerator for a snack. "The teacher came up to me this afternoon," he said, his voice muffled by the family Frigidaire. "And she asked me if it was real hard being new."

"That was it?" his mother asked. "She asked you if it was hard being new?"

"Well, sure, Mom," her son answered. "What else would it be but hard?"

His mother knew instant gratitude—a warm and thankful flood of it washing from her scalp down to her toes. Her gratitude was for this as yet faceless teacher who had recognized and understood her son's feelings, and more important, had communicated that as acceptance of *him*.

"It is hard," his mother agreed, "sometimes very hard."

"Yeah," her son replied, flashing her a familiar grin around the refrigerator door. "But it'll get better, Mom. Don't worry."

I know this story well. Oh, how I know it! It is my son's story, and it is mine. And I thank God for the accepting love of good teachers who are there when I, a mother, cannot be.

Love Defined: Unconditional Acceptance

Acceptance is the heart of love. It is the requisite, the foundation for everything that follows. My son's wise and compassionate teacher demonstrated acceptance of a child's natural feelings of worry and insecurity in the face of the unknown. She welcomed him by recognizing his feelings. She took him just the way he was and told him he was perfectly legitimate that way. In fact, my son's battle was won when the teacher simply stretched out her hand.

The reason a communication of acceptance is so important to the teacher/student relationship is that it is what Christ models for us. He accepts us for what we are and loves us right where we are, whether we change for the better or for the worse or whether we never change at all. If we had to earn that kind of love, we never could. No human being deserves it, but we are not given that love from God because we deserve it. We are given it because we *are*. What wonderful lovers of children teachers could be if we communicated to them the same gentle acceptance Christ shows to us!

Contemporary society, however, does not accept people the way they are. "Progress is our most important product," brags Madison Avenue. Products must be new and improved, and according to advertisers, people are products too. We have to be shampooed, cleansed, sprayed, lacquered, aerated, toned up, trimmed down, deodorized, sanforized, and homogenized in order to be "marketable" commodities—to be, in a word, *acceptable*.

And as far as "love" itself goes, our air-waves are inundated with the modern sounds of it. We are told to "let your baby come and love you." In fact, the songwriters intimate we should beg for it, over and over: "baby, baby, baby." To cacophonous backgrounds, we hear "I dreamed of being the one" and "she is the one," or "he's my lover" and "I love him so." We find out about the heartbreak and rejection, the jealousy and anger of "love." In the popular culture of our day, love is a worrisome commodity that is likely to be withheld without warning.

But the Christian perspective on love is very different from the world's. The Christian perspective says, "I will love you whether you drive that expensive car or not, whether you have

dandruff or not, whether you wear this perfume or that after-
shave, and, furthermore, I will love you even if you never love
me back."

Love between a husband and wife in Christian marriage gives
us some idea of what love is like in general. The analogy carries
over to schools, as we shall see. Scripture defines the love of a
husband for his wife in terms of Christ's love for the church
(Eph. 5:22–33). It shows itself through giving, encouragement,
concern, and commitment.

First, the way a person gives defines that person's love for
another. *Agape* love is the highest form of love in this regard,
because its basis is totally unselfish giving. This love meets the
need of another, even at the expense of self-need. The second
characteristic of love—encouragement—helps facilitate the development of another so that he or she might be what God
intended him or her to be, while the third characteristic, concern, is the cherishing, or protective, aspect of love. Commitment, the fourth aspect of love found in the Ephesians passage,
relates to being bound to another by free choice, to a guarantee,
to an assurance or promise that the lover will always be there for
the beloved. These four qualities that Christ demonstrates to
believers are the same ones a husband is to provide his wife—
and a teacher could do well to provide her or his students with
this demonstration too.

In this same passage from Ephesians, we see respect for the
lover as being the responsibility of the one who is loved. Respect
is nothing more than a genuine response to being loved. And
who wouldn't respond with respect for the lover if surrounded
by the kind of love Christ gives his church? Teachers in school
classrooms would rarely have to worry about getting the respect
they want from their students if they demonstrated love
through the mediums of giving, encouragement, concern, and
commitment!

In his book *The Four Loves*, C. S. Lewis divides love in human
relationships into the categories of affection, friendship, *eros*,
and charity. Before discussing any of them, Lewis warns that

sentimental literature has not done love any favors, elevating it in some ways above God himself, as if love were a god in its own right. Still, to examine love is helpful. While we can't "see light . . . by light we can see things." As Lewis, and we, examine the underpinnings of love in its many forms, we see this common thread running throughout all of its manifestations: acceptance of the person being loved. With love, there is no struggle to "change" a person. Acceptance of the beloved undergirds all of love's forms. "In God there is no hunger that needs to be filled," writes Lewis, "only plenteousness that desires to give." Children aren't in schools for teachers; teachers are in schools for children.

Christ's story of the prodigal son (Luke 15:11–32) is a familiar one. Since familiarity sometimes closes our minds—as if we've already "heard it all"—we must be careful not to overlook Christ's essential teaching. Bible commentaries tell us that of all the parables Jesus told, the story of the prodigal son comes closest to giving us a glimpse of the gentle face of God. It shows God's love as going beyond justice, beyond reason. No matter what the son did, no matter how foolish or ridiculous his actions, no matter that others might scorn him, his father continued to love him. That does not mean the father did not suffer and hurt for his son, or did not in fact agonize over some of the bad decisions his son made. But it does mean the father loved just because the son *was*. The son did not have to earn that love. He only had to *be*.

How we need to make sure that children in today's world know this!—that they see the gentle face of God in the faces of the adults nearest to them. Too many haven't the scantest idea that there is such a love possible in the world.

The word *acceptance* has some wonderful synonyms that show its freeing nature: recognition, belief, affirmation, endorsement, "stamp of approval." The antonyms, not surprisingly, give the opposite feeling: rejection, repudiation, disapproval, disavowal. It is grim, indeed, to not feel accepted.

Knowing that others accept us provides every one of us with

something very important: the chance to be happy, content, at peace with the world we live in and with the people around us. Children have little control over what happens to them, over those of life's episodes that can make them either confident and content or dreadfully despairing. They need a foundation of love that depends on nothing except the fact that they *are,* a love that requires nothing from them, that asks nothing in return, that assures them they are perfectly fine just the way they are.

Love, through acceptance, allows us to have confidence in our own basic God-given nature. It is a shield against the forces of the world over which we can exercise no control. "And his banner over me is love" (Song of Sol. 2:4, NIV). The world would be a very different place for children, far less threatening, far friendlier—indeed, far happier—if we could communicate this kind of fully accepting love to them.

Seeking Approval: The Exhausting Quest to "Earn" Love

Today's world is a distressing place in which to grow up. Young people have many fears about coping with it. Not the least of these fears is that they might be "unlovable." They fear they are not pretty or handsome enough, they fear they are too skinny or (more commonly) not skinny enough. They fear they are too unmanly or unfeminine to attract the interest of the opposite sex. They fear they aren't bright enough, that they will do or say something stupid. They worry that they "are not like everyone else." What if everyone else already knows the answer to the question they want to ask? What if, after full growth, they turn out to be shorter than everybody else? What if their hair is curly instead of straight, or straight instead of curly? What if everyone else's skin clears up but theirs?

These fears, particularly among adolescents, are real and sometimes overwhelming. But they are also natural fears, apprehensions we have each experienced as we risked growing toward full maturity. Despite the fact that going through these doubts is a normal part of growing up, we cannot laugh them off lightly and say to our children, "Don't worry. You'll live." Nobody appreciates being taken less than seriously.

As we saw in the last chapter, the best teaching is modeling. Just so, the best way to demonstrate to kids that the condition of their hair or their musculature, that their ability to be elected class president or to win the lead in the play makes no difference to us is to *show* them that it really makes no difference. We do not alter our behavior toward them when they look or perform particularly well. (This does not mean, of course, that we do not offer sincere compliments. But the thrust of most of these compliments should relate to character and inner being, and not to accomplishments.) Unfortunately, in our urge to help children grow we often unwittingly compound the normal stresses of growing up by unspoken messages about what gains our approval.

There is a delicate balance to strike between loving children as they are and encouraging them to reach their potential. We will deal with the second part—the encouragement of potential—in chapters 4 and 5. What is important to realize at present is that reaching inside yourself and calling up what is there is impossible until you are certain you will be loved even if you fail. And such reassurance is developmental. Our children have to "grow" into knowledge of our love for them, a love that is freed from anything they can do to earn it, as we demonstrate by our actions. Indeed, they cannot earn it.

In the scheme of basic needs on Maslow's hierarchy, to love and be loved comes before the need to be respected. Knowing that you are loved is necessary before you can strive to accomplish those things which other people admire. If we push children into achievement before they have under them the firm foundation of our complete acceptance, we are pressuring them through developmental stages for which they not ready. We are dumping a load of stress on them through the sending of contradictory messages. We may be saying, "I love you," or even, "It's all right that you're not the best hitter on the team,"

but our compulsive behavior as adult care-givers can say something quite different if we shriek and go crazy when they hit a
home run but are loudly silent when they strike out. Nonverbal
messages are stronger than verbal ones.

Let me illustrate this another way. *Newsweek* magazine calls
the "Kindergarten Is Too Late!" movement the new ABCs of
babyhood: Anxiety, Betterment, Competition. Today's parents
are older, richer, more combative, and "firmly convinced that
there are lessons for everything." Contemporary parents have
put off having children until later in life when their careers are
firmly established, and they bring much of their sense of ag-
gressiveness in personal achievement to their parenting role. As
Dr. Berry Brazelton, a Harvard pediatrician, says, "Everyone
wants to raise the smartest kid in America rather than the best
adjusted, happiest kid." Even Dr. Spock, the oracle by whose
precepts many of today's parents were themselves raised, warns,
"Being persuaded that the most important thing is to be bright
and get good grades may move people away from the natural,
emotional ways of dealing with life." Psychologist Lee Salk says
more flatly yet, "This pressure for high achievement really sets
children up for failure. Love should be unconditional where
children are concerned; it should not be based on I.Q."[1]

Anything else is carrying the rat race into the nursery. Implications for children's feelings of self-worth—or for what self-
worth is based on—are devastating. Thus, we help mold the
personalities of children who gnaw their fingernails down to the
quick and then worry that they are no longer lovable because
their hands are unsightly. "Superficiality," Richard Foster has
written, "is the curse of our age."[2]

These social phenomena are not just associated with the children of working mothers and fathers. Parenting pressures infect
those mothers who stay at home as well, though perhaps they
are subtler, and so less recognizable. For both mothers who
never worked and those who quit work to take up full-time
parenting, the child may become the symbol of the mother's

worth. The pressure on children is excruciating under any of these circumstances.

One Chicago psychologist has seen several distressed two- and three-year-olds who have pulled out clumps of hair or their eyelashes. Other signs of disturbance may not surface for years. *Anorexia nervosa* often develops in teenagers raised in homes that rank intellectual achievement above all else. In its first five years of operation, the Theraplay Institute in Chicago saw some 3,000 troubled youngsters ten years old and younger. The clinical director at the institute says, "We give parents *permission* to enjoy their child and to love him for what he is, not who he can be" (italics mine).[3] Have we gotten to a point in our society where permission must be given to parents to love their children?

Through every good intention to help a child succeed, teachers can also apply this same kind of pressure. Pressure to perform, to finish assignments, and to "do your best" is very common and potentially devastating. If a child does not succeed, parents are called, and the school and home get together—a united front—to add still more pressure. Now the child has not just one problem to deal with; he or she has two. There seems no escape, no one left who loves the child whether the work is done or not.

A wise and warm teacher friend of mind was telling me about her son who at age fourteen experienced a great deal of stomach distress. He was hospitalized for tests, and for awhile there was a grim possibility that he had pancreatic cancer. Mother and son discussed it with each other, directly and forthrightly, as they awaited the medical diagnosis. He could die. They knew it. It was right there in front of them.

Fortunately, the tests did not reveal the disease they most feared, and three years later my friend said to me, "You know, I decided right then never again to nag him about something I knew I wouldn't even be mentioning if he had only a few months to live. Now I ask myself, 'If I was about to lose him, would that seem important to say?' When the answer is no, he

never hears the advice or the motherly sermon I might otherwise have delivered."

I think it is important to reveal to you the context in which I
heard this story. It was in a teacher-parent conference. I was the
parent. My teacher friend, whose story this is, shared it with me
in an effort to help me understand some of the pressure I was
unwittingly putting on my own son, her stressed-out student.
And now, in case you might need to hear it too, I pass it on.

Christ: Love's Glorious Manifestation

"Live a life of love, just as Christ loved us and gave himself up
for us as a fragrant offering and sacrifice to God" (Eph. 5:2,
NIV). Because Christ could give his life for us in love, we can
give ours to others. Paul writes it is his prayer that "you, together with all God's people, may have the power to understand
how broad and long, how high and deep, is Christ's love. Yes,
may you come to know his love—although it can never be fully
known—and so be completely filled with the very nature of
God" (Eph. 3:18–19, TEV).

With that kind of love, love that is broad and long, high and
deep, we cannot fail to make a difference in children's lives.
Christ, who loves you and me, makes it possible for us to love
others. Those others, our students, can in their turn love still
others.

We cannot always know the names of the students our love
influences. Sometimes the students we influence are not even in
our classrooms. Sometimes they are passers-by in the hall or
lunchroom. Sometimes, as we have already seen, they are not in
schools at all. We frequently are not aware when we have
influenced lives, much less which ones. In that sense, many
children who cross our paths remain strangers to us—and we to
them. But that's quite all right. It is being strangers in the
friendliest sense. A placard I once saw in an ice cream parlor

read: THERE ARE NO STRANGERS HERE, ONLY FRIENDS WE
HAVE NOT MET.

Christ increases our understanding of love in much the same
way. His love was filled with the power of tenderness, so much
so that we still experience it today. Yet we never knew him "in
the flesh." We never saw or touched him as did his disciples.
We were strangers to him in this sense, yet we are strangers
who have become intimate friends, who indeed know his love
"firsthand." Reinhold Niebuhr wrote in *Faith and History* that
"man must realize himself not within himself but in a responsible and loving relation to his fellowmen."[4]

We have already seen Jesus as the Model of teaching. He
taught by giving himself. In fact, he gave himself so completely
that he demonstrated a quality of love that is basic to our study:
human beings have intrinsic value, not because of their goodness, but because their being testifies to God as Creator. By
accepting us as we are, by becoming like us, Christ underscores
our complete brotherhood with him. He is Love Incarnate.

When we acknowledge the greatness of his love and are
about the process of returning it, we must not feel a pressure to
be perfect, as he was. Rather, what is essential to remember is
that we are *forgiven*. There is no pressure when we recognize
acceptance as the basic foundation of Christ's love. Indeed,
acceptance enables, whereas pressure to become different, or
"better," cripples. Acceptance is the forgiving quality of love. If
love were to insist on perfection, it would destroy rather than
save.

Scripture is so filled with references to God's love and to
Christ's demonstration of that love to us that it is impossible to
cite them all within a short chapter. One concordance has nearly 500 verses from the New Testament listed as being specific
teachings on love from Christ's life. Christ was the greatest
human lover the world has ever known. In his loving, he teaches
how to love. So here is the answer to the world's quandary
about what love is: "Love comes from God. Everyone who loves

has been born of God and knows God. Whoever does not love does not know God, because God is love. This is how God showed his love among us: He sent his one and only Son into the world that we might live through him. This is love: not that we loved God, *but that he loved us*" (1 John 4:7–10, NIV, italics mine).

He loved us, and yet we know ourselves to be unworthy of a love that complete. We didn't earn it (and we can't); we don't deserve it and are, therefore, not really entitled to it. But we have it nonetheless. And that is the legacy Christ left for us to communicate in classrooms and everywhere. He left us a model of how to be a lover: acceptance of people just the way they are, warts and all.

Some people (including some children) don't seem particularly lovable. In *A Girl Named Sooner,* novelist Suzanne Clauser introduces us to an orphaned waif covered with grime and sores, a child who has little or no familiarity with soap or toothpaste or toilet paper. It is in this condition that Sooner is brought before Elizabeth, her prospective adoptive mother. Elizabeth recoils from the child, horrified and repulsed. "Nobody could be expected to love such a child," Clauser writes. "And nobody will find fault with Elizabeth, not even Elizabeth, if she couldn't."[5] But Elizabeth learns to love even the unlovable and, in her loving, discovers Sooner wasn't so unlovable after all.

Christ looks beyond the dirt and grime with which we are all covered, and into our very hearts. He loves what we are, whether he likes what he sees on the surface or not. He loves us in spite of the filth. He sees what's beneath it, and that's what he smiles upon. "A plant must have roots below as well as sunlight above and roots must be grubby," writes C. S. Lewis. "Much of the grubbiness is clean dirt if only you will leave it in the garden and not keep sprinkling it over the library table."[6] If attention is overly focused on our qualities of grubbiness, rather than on those of our loveliness, confidence that we are lovable beings soon disappears. Christ accepts us because we are created in God's image. We are testimony to that creation. That is enough for Christ. And through him, but only through him, it can be enough for all of us who are care-givers to children.

Misunderstood Humanism: What It Really Means in Education

Christians sometimes criticize the public schools for being institutions that advocate secular humanism. While there is a branch of educational psychology labeled *humanism,* it is in no way related to what is commonly referred to as "secular humanism." Let me explain.

"Secular humanism" is the belief that within all people is the power to overcome any adversity. It is the belief that, if we can but call on them, our own resources will carry us through every situation. We have, it is said, what it takes inside of us to overcome anything. In this belief, there is little or no room for God. From a secular humanist point of view, we do not have to rely on God. We have only to rely on ourselves.

While we do not use the capacities we are given (most of us, for instance, use only 10 percent of our brain power; Einstein is thought to have used 13 percent), nevertheless this "calling up of our own human resources" is, in no way, what humanism means in educational terms. Untapped potential is there, but the potential itself is a gift from God. We cannot separate our humanness from him. Humanism in classrooms is more accurately defined as a way to look at each person as a distinctly separate and individually complex human being. Humanism is seeing the particularity of another.

In this context, classroom humanism is not only compatible with Christian perspective, it *is* Christian perspective. We must not let the term "humanism" fool us into believing otherwise. Perhaps what we need is a new term, one that rubs out the root word "human" altogether.

On the other hand, if we actually were to rid ourselves of the word "human," we would ignore what is so wonderful about Christ's example: how to be *authentically* human. There is no

shame in using the word. There is only confusion in our interpretation of what it means. In truth, we need "human" in
our vocabulary in order to understand fully what it was that
Christ did and continues to do. He came in *human* form and,
through it, he experienced all that is human about us. He knows
us intimately and loves us through the knowing.

What proponents of humanistic education, or being human
in the classroom, suggest is that teachers, first and foremost,
should be *learning facilitators,* and that to be such, teachers
must be genuine, accepting, and empathetic. That is all such
humanism is, in its very unthreatening reality. The human race,
to which so many of us belong (as G. K. Chesterton quite as-
tutely pointed out), must, ironically, continually exhort itself to
be human. It is the "exhorting to be human" that educational
humanism is all about. We will look more at this educational
view of human functioning later in our study. For now, though,
the mystery of what humanism really is needs to be clarified so
we can get on with the business of looking at teachers as lovers
within a humanistic framework.

Being Humane: Treating Children as People

Examples abound from school classrooms of teachers offering
love, and unfortunately, examples also abound of teachers offering apathy or hostility. It is valuable to look at some of each type.
Through them, we can see how a humane view of students as
individuals communicates love and how an "inhumane" view
doesn't.

Twelve-year-old Matt has lost his permission slip for a field
trip soon to be taken by his class. His teacher demands to know
where it is. Matt replies that he guesses it's lost. His teacher says
he'd better bring it if he wants to go on the trip. Matt wonders
aloud how he can do that since he doesn't know where it is.
Instead of giving him another slip or contacting his parents in an
effort to help him solve this familiar dilemma, the teacher tells

Matt he'd better think of something or he won't be going with the rest of the class.

Message Matt "heard": You are definitely not my favorite kid. In fact, all I needed was a reason to leave you behind. Thank you for giving it to me, since I wasn't looking forward to taking you with us anyway.

Humane or inhumane?

It is show-and-tell time, and Melinda, the student currently showing and telling, has just had a birthday. She has received as a birthday gift a fancy little gizmo that unfolds, does this and that, and whirs and clicks and spins. She has brought it tenderly to school and has carefully laid it out on the rug for her classmates to see. Melinda talks in a quiet voice, perhaps not expecting anyone to listen because certainly no one is listening. Not needing Melinda's gizmo to do it for them, the rest of the children are buzzing and whirring at their seats and basically ignoring the whole show-and-tell scene. The teacher, at her desk grading papers, never looks up while Melinda shares her treasure. Melinda packs up her birthday present, refolding and tucking it as carefully as she'd undone it, and returns to her seat, head down. As if on cue, the teacher finally glances up. "Anyone else?" this teacher asks crisply. Another tentative hand comes up. The teacher nods at the hand raiser and bends over her grading again.

Message Melinda and her classmates "heard": Nothing Melinda says is more important than what I'm doing. In fact, I find it so unimportant, I really don't see why anyone would want to listen. Frankly, I'm sure if you follow my lead, you'll agree.

Humane or inhumane?

Jason, an advanced art student, is learning how to do linoleum prints. He is painstakingly carving a many-masted sailing ship out of his block. Encountering a difficulty, he asks his art instructor a question about how to get this and thus just so. Helpful and caring, and entirely oblivious to the message about to be sent, the instructor takes the linoleum block from Jason and proceeds to answer the question by doing the technique for him. Jason watches helplessly. His block returned to him, the technique in question having been completed, Jason sags—but not so that anyone who wasn't watching would notice.

Message Jason "heard": You'll probably just mess it up if I tell you how to do it, so I better do it myself. Then we can be sure it'll look nice rather than inept.

Humane or inhumane?

A special guest is coming to the classroom, a guest the class has been looking forward to having come for a time. One of the students, Stephanie, discovers she has to be gone the afternoon the visitor is to arrive. A distant relative has died, requiring her to leave at noon in order to go out of town for the funeral. Recognizing Stephanie's disappointment at being absent when the guest is scheduled, the teacher packs a brown paper bag and labels it, "Survival Kit for the Trip," handing it over to Stephanie as her parents arrive to pick her up from school. After being deposited in the backseat of the family car, Stephanie opens up the bag and discovers a paperback book, a box of raisins, and a fat pack of sugarless bubble gum.

Message Stephanie "heard": I recognize your disappointment at missing something we all planned for, but I want you to know I care about you and am thinking of you. Come back as soon as you can. I'll be here, waiting.

Ah, now, inhumane or *humane?*

These are some of the ways a focus on the individuality, or the *personhood,* of students can communicate love or a withholding of love. There are other ways too.

Acknowledgment of Feelings: Its Lasting Impact

Lori, a college student of mine, wasn't certain at age five if her life was ever going to get off the ground. Somehow she has totally blocked kindergarten from her mind, but first grade was, in her estimation, probably even worse. "The sad thing is," she says, "I remember it well. My teacher was pregnant and always sick, so she didn't come to school much. I had a lot of substitutes that year, but none of them stayed long enough to benefit the class."

Then second grade came, and Lori had hopes that it would be better. Amazingly, she had not lost her eagerness for school. But she grew to hate it during this second grade year. The teacher singled out the more shy students to answer questions. She didn't want them "getting out of something." The trick was to put up your hand; if you did not, you were called on. Lori did not. She was shy and painfully embarrassed when her name was called, which usually effectively wiped out her memory for the answer to whatever question was currently being asked.

The teacher quit before the year was out, and Lori was trans-ferred to another room. By this time, she says, "I was apathetic about school, to say the least." But then, she goes on, "a miracle walked into my new classroom."

The new teacher, a quiet Christian woman who was content first to accept instead of change her students, spent a great deal of time with Lori, assessing her needs and then fulfilling them. At one point, this teacher said to her new student, "Lori, it is not your fault that you hate school, and your feelings are not wrong. But we are going to work together and see what hap-pens." Once Lori felt accepted, she was free to grow.

Lori picks up the story again. "I knew this lady really cared about me. She wanted to help. And she even came to school every day! As a result of her attention, I caught up with my peers and eased into third grade. Even as a second grader, I realized the teacher *does* make the difference."

And Lori is now working hard to prepare herself to be a teacher, a teacher who plans to be accepting, to be consistent in her attendance at school, and to "make a difference."

Melanie, a student of mine also planning to teach, recalls Miss Hobrock, her first grade teacher. Melanie was tremen-dously shy, as Lori was, and asked nothing more out of life than to not be noticed. But Miss Hobrock noticed her anyway. One time, in Melanie's words, "she gave me a present—a ceramic vase with little flowers in it. That vase took a special place in my room at home, and I cherished it very much."

The gift symbolized something to a tiny first grade girl: her worth. She was worth a vase of flowers. Yet she had done nothing to earn it. In fact, if anything, she had done the op-posite—she had been so painfully shy (and being noticed *was* pain to Melanie) that she "should" have been very unlovable indeed. There was nothing sparkly or overtly charming about her.

Miss Hobrock, however, didn't see it that way. She made school a warm and friendly and especially loving place for a timid little girl. The gift was an outward manifestation that demonstrated very well Miss Hobrock's valuing of the distinct individual in her room. It was a way to get a handle on encour-agement, a way to see it in the "flesh."

Melanie smiles when she recalls this, something that hap-pened a great many years ago but is remembered instantly. "I still have that vase," Melanie says today, "and it always re-minds me of Miss Hobrock and the special affection between us."

Karla, another student studying to be a teacher, remembers in eighth grade when her grandmother died how her teacher that year proved himself to be a very special friend indeed. "He talked to me about the death of his own grandmother and some of the feelings he'd gone through. This helped me realize that what I was feeling was normal." But it was typical of him, Karla recalls, to be personal with his class. "He often would tell us stories about things he had done at our age and mistakes that he'd made. This made him a real person to us." "Since the children have flesh and blood, he too shared in their human-ity. . ." (Heb. 2:14, NIV).

In *To Kill a Mockingbird,* novelist Harper Lee records this brief but important piece of advice from a father to his daughter:

"First of all," he said, "if you can learn a simple trick, Scout, you'll get along a lot better with all kinds of folks. You never really understand a person until you consider things from his point of view—"

"Sir?"

"—until you climb into his skin and walk around in it."[7]

Friendship: Adults and Children Together

An Arabian proverb describes friendship as acceptance: "A friend is one to whom one may pour out all the contents of one's heart, chaff and grain together, knowing that the gentlest of hands will take and sift it, keep what is worth keeping and, with the breath of kindness, blow the rest away."

Friends accept you just the way you are and never judge you for what you are not. A friend does not request that you change. A friend does not deny what you are, but instead, takes you right where you are and shares that moment with you. Teachers are often called friends, and so they are if they can communicate friendship through the love of gentle acceptance.

A child I care for very much, my youngest son, was telling me one afternoon when he got home from school about a particular teacher. "You know," he said with weary insight, from his position of collapse on the floor, "she doesn't treat us all the same, and that's good. But what's bad is she's the one who decides what you're like. You don't get to decide for yourself." He sighed, his eyes staring dully up at the ceiling of our home, as he went resignedly on, "And then she treats you the way she's decided you are." I believe I can say, with some measure of certainty, that if my normally perceptive son is right, this teacher is not a lover to children. And if she is not a lover, she is not a friend.

Ernest Boyer, principal author of "The Carnegie Report," reminds us to "recognize that the school is a connected institution."[8] It is this connectedness with other forces in the community which gives it its strength and power to influence lives in important ways. (The idea of connectedness is one very good reason why Christian community leaders should involve themselves in what happens in public schools.)

Connectedness is a force at work in all relationships. In fact, it is probably redundant to say "connectedness" and "friendship," for they are the warp and woof of the same cloth. We are all "connected" to other human beings in some manner, and it is this interweaving of lives that gives birth to friendship. But we are sometimes strung or webbed together with such gossamer lines that we do not always notice them. Even so, they are there.

Reassurance: The Need for Daily Infusions

We have been focusing in this chapter on the importance of loving children. But if we surround children with too many visible reminders of our love, won't it go to their heads? Can't we "accept" them just a little too much for their own good? From the paucity of the reminders in many homes and schools, it would seem a great many adults are overly concerned about a child's opportunity to achieve humility. They withhold outward expressions of love. Are some of us saying, in effect, that it is okay to *feel* love for a child but not to *show* it?

Charlotte's Web tackles this dilemma in a beautiful way. The story of this children's classic is about miracles and friendship. Miracles occur in Zuckerman's barn and within a remarkable spider's web. Lives are saved, commitments made, relationships knitted together for all time and into succeeding generations because those relationships are seen as being worth all the effort they take. Charlotte, through diligence and industry, devotes herself entirely to her friendship for Wilbur and never deviates from her philosophy of love, even though it costs her her life. White tells us that "some of Wilbur's friends in the barn worried for fear all this attention would go to his head and make him stuck up. But it never did. . . . He realized that friendship is one of the most satisfying things in the world."

The reason for reassurance, though, goes beyond mere knowledge that it won't go to a child's head. Reassurance is at the very heart of love. Our ability to face the world is dependent on our belief that we are lovable. And it is other people's responses to us that lead us toward this belief. An anonymous little verse reminds us of the need for reassurance:

> Do you love me
> Or do you not?
> You told me once
> But I forgot.

All people have the desire to know they are loved. "All people" includes you and me. We may grow weary of reassuring others of our love for *them,* but we don't want them to cease telling us that *we* are loved. Anyone who is married knows a marriage would have a difficult time surviving if the last time we heard our husband or wife say "I love you" was at the altar. And what if it was the last time we were hugged or kissed by our spouse? Do we just take it on faith that love endures when there are no outward displays of it? Hardly. We grow increasingly insecure and frightened.

Children need daily doses of love, too. They need to be cuddled and tucked in at night (age really knows no limits on this). They need to have their hair rumpled and "I love you, I love you, I love you" murmured against their cheek. They need it gently traced onto their arm with our fingernails when we are sitting beside them. Indeed, children need *lots* of the right kind of touching.

We need to be showering our children with reminders of the depth of our love: notes tucked into lunches, among the clean socks in dresser drawers, under the toilet seat lid or the bedspread. I know a teacher who, at Easter, had an egg hunt with pop-apart plastic eggs. Into these eggs this teacher had inserted all kinds of different messages, such as: "I think you are absolutely one terrific kid!" and "How was I ever so lucky to get you in my class?" I know another teacher who took out a classified ad in the local newspaper on Valentine's Day which read: "Mrs. Johnson loves every person in her class." Following this were the first names of each of her students.

Children need expressions of affection *when* they least expect it too, and in *ways* they don't expect. A few years ago our youngest son, Kyle, was badly bitten on the face by a dog. The dog's jaws caught him from lip to nose to lower eyelid to eyebrow. We still don't know why his face wasn't ripped away, but it wasn't. Nevertheless, he was hospitalized with a severe infection, and there was much concern that the infection might travel into his brain. He was swollen beyond recognition, he was terrified (so were his father and I), he was hooked around the clock to an I.V., and he was kept in isolation. It was not a happy time in our family history.

His teacher that year, a wonderful individual named Mamie, came to see Kyle in the hospital. As her husband and my husband and I talked in one corner of the room, Mamie spent nearly forty minutes next to Kyle's bed, stroking his one exposed arm, up and back, speaking to him in a hushed and intimate voice. His eyes never left hers. I don't know to this day what she told him. I have always felt it an intrusion to ask. But I do know that when she left, she reached down and kissed him right on his unrecognizable, infected face. She accepted him the way he was, and she told him so. He was not repulsive to her. She loved him, and that was that. Her demonstration of love meant far more to him than mine did. Mine was expected. I was his mother; I was supposed to support him in time of crisis. But Mamie was his teacher, and her uplifting of him came to him as a delightful surprise.

Love: The Gift of Confidence

Emily Dickinson's inimitable poetry speaks thoughtfully and truly:

> "A word is dead
> When it is said,"
> Some say.
> I say it just
> Begins to live
> That day.

Kyle has never forgotten Mamie's visit to him in the hospital. He remembers her stroking and kissing him when he was his foulest. Neither has he forgotten that she loved him. Her acceptance of him has gotten him through some rough days when other teachers have not behaved so lovingly. But through the years he has been able to believe in his heart that Mamie could not have been wrong about him—else why would she have done the things she did?— and so her love has sustained him. She was, and is, his good and true friend. "Once you are Real," the Skin Horse wisely tells the Velveteen Rabbit in Margery Williams's classic story, "you can't be ugly, except to people who don't understand."

Barb, one of my college students, remembers Mrs. Wooten, a teacher who was, Barb tells me, "a wonderful friend, helper, and listener." In particular, Barb recalls a time in high school when she had great apprehensions and doubts about her future. Where should she go to college? What should she major in? There were so many forebodings running rampant through Barb's brain that she did not know how to articulate them all. But "I could express my fear of leaving home and not having any friends to Mrs. Wooten. She told me that *she* was my friend and that she would be thinking about me." Barb smiles in grateful remembrance, adding, "The day I graduated from high school she whispered in my ear, 'I'll be praying for you, Barb.' Just knowing that she cared meant so much to me."

When I was in seventh and eighth grade my English teacher was a fascinating lady named Katie Kallini. Her names fits her. It reminds me of energy and laughter. I can almost sing it: KAY-tee Ka-LEE-nee. For years she was Mrs. Kallini to me. No more. She has become just "Katie" now. Katie is, pure and simple, the reason I became a teacher.

Katie is a tall, slender, perpetually smiling woman. When I was first her student, her hair was dark and bobbed, swinging loose and clean about her cheekbones. She wears the same style, but her hair is white now. The smile has not changed.

Katie spent a good portion of her professional life as a teacher in the Philippines and Japan. She had fascinating stories to tell us and a vast command of the vocabulary with which to tell them. As her student, I felt she loved me in particular. I know now that she did love me, but not in particular. It was just that I loved *her* in particular, because she was so eminently accepting of me. Acceptance was her style. She is a lady of *great* style!

Sometimes during those two years in which I was her student, Katie would not come to school. Not much was said to us about her absences, but it was always disappointing when she wasn't there. In fact, it was hard for me emotionally to get through those days when she was gone. During these same junior-high years, another teacher in the building had advised my best friend to stay away from me; I was a "bad influence" and my friend was "too good" for me—whatever that meant. Katie was my insurance against having to believe such things.

When Katie would return from these protracted absences, she would get around with the aid of a walker, a metal contraption that she would have to set down carefully with her arms before being able to painfully move her feet. She would go through this laborious process every time she wanted to take a step. It was her courageous route to regaining full mobility. I can still see her going down the hallways of Jonas Salk School in her halting but determined manner, a smile and a greeting for every student on her lips.

The initials "M.S." were whispered, but I really had no idea then what "M.S." meant. I knew it was a recurring disease, and I dreaded its attacks for Katie, but I was ignorant about what it did to her besides leaving her dependent on a walker. Otherwise, when she returned to our class, she was the same.

After I went to high school, Katie and her husband Tad moved out of the area where I lived, but we stayed in touch. We were consummate pen pals. In fact, we were pen pals for the next twenty-five years. We never lost touch with each other. Katie had loved me, and I had "stayed loved." I was free to be normal and natural with her, because she liked me the way I was. She has been proud of the direction my life has taken, delighted by and supportive of many things, and yet I know none of my accomplishments has had an impact on her love for me. She accepted me into her heart when my main achievement seemed nothing more than "earning" another teacher's assessment that I was unfit to be near. It has been so freeing through the years to know Katie's love is not dependent on anything I do.

We always said we wanted to get back together again, but for many reasons it kept not working out. Sometimes her letters mentioned her "old friend," meaning multiple sclerosis, but she never dwelt on it nor responded much when I asked. And I was busy with babies and going to graduate school. The miles and our differing lifestyles kept us apart.

Finally, well into my late thirties, with two children as big as myself and a husband in tow, I arrived on Katie's doorstep. Her husband Tad greeted us warmly, hugged us (I had hardly known Tad, as Katie did not know my family) and ushered us inside a home filled with mementos of their world travels. After twenty-five years of waiting, I was at Katie's house.

But I learned she was, once again, hospitalized with her "old friend." It was the first recurrence that year, and Katie had not wanted me told for fear I would change my mind about coming. Our long-awaited reunion had to take place beside a hospital bed, but the person in the bed was still Katie. She regaled my children with stories of when I had been her student—an adolescent younger than they were—and we all laughed and wept and blessed the name of friendship, the tie that forever binds. Indeed, the love of unconditional acceptance—a love that does not ask for straight A's or anything else—is needed in classrooms and homes if we dare hope that our children and ourselves "shall be like him" (1 John 3:2, NIV).

CHAPTER THREE

Do You Know There Are Hurtful
Things I Can't Tell You?

THE NEED FOR HEALERS

I have lived a great deal among grown-ups.
I have seen them intimately, close at hand.
And that hasn't much improved
my opinion of them.

—Antoine de Saint Exupéry—

Item: A group of hikers in the Rocky Mountains hears a child's cries coming from an outhouse. Bewildered, they look down into the pit under the toilet opening and see a three-year-old girl ankle-deep in sewage. Too shocked and horrified to think with coherence, the hikers ask inanely what she is doing down there. The tiny girl, whom we will call Susan, replies, "I'm home. I live here."

Item: A teacher persists in addressing one of her students as "William" even though his given name is "Willie." She explains her practice to colleagues by telling them that this boy's name *should* have been William. Indeed, if his parents weren't so ignorant, his name *would* have been William. By correcting the parents' mistake, she is doing her duty as a teacher. "Willie is not a proper name," she says in calm reply to questions.

Item: Denae, an eleven-year-old girl, is in charge of fixing dinner for herself and her three younger siblings every evening after school. The parents, one of whom is an alcoholic and one of whom works the late shift, are not home when their children are. Denae is given a small amount of food money to help with the task of feeding the family. Most nights Denae solves this culinary problem by purchasing two or three large bags of potato chips. In front of a flickering television set, the children feast on an evening meal of potato chips until their stomachs are full.

Difficult as it may be to believe, each of these three stories is true. Actually, each of these stories is mild compared to what many children endure. Child abuse is on the rise. Physical abuse, including sexual abuse, is reported with ever-increasing frequency. Psychological abuse, on the other hand, often goes undetected, and thus, unreported. Another dimension of child abuse is neglect, which is difficult to prove as well. Even though agencies set up by law to protect children may, in fact, not always be able to carry out their responsibilities, Christians in public schools can make a difference to Susan and Willie and Denae and all the others who are in desperate need of healing. Because of the power imbued in us by God, we can and must provide children in schools with something they might otherwise not receive.

Childhood's Erosion: Subtle but Dangerous Abuse

The beginning three examples are exactly that—a place for us to begin our path toward awareness of what is happening to too many children. There are all kinds of troublesome hurts in children's lives which ultimately can lead to everything from insecurity to suicide. Educator Benjamin Bloom has noted that "[a doctor] may say, 'These [patients] are going to die and these are going to live.' But the question he should be asking is, 'What can I do about the patient's present condition?' "[1] In order to do anything about "the patient's present condition," we first have to recognize it.

Outright, appalling abuse we do recognize. Indeed, it is diffi-

cult to miss. Sadistic adults taking out their reprehensible im-
pulses on children sicken not only us. Such people are scorned
even by hardened criminals. In penitentiaries, the lives most
endangered by the wrath of other inmates are those of convicted
child molesters.

While it is a sad truth that many youngsters fall victim to
psychopaths, we must not become too complacent regarding our
own innocence. We need to realize, in fact, that some blows are
dealt by us. To be sure, our contributions to the problem are
mostly subtle, but potentially they are just as destructive. What
we do is mete out severe, often debilitating, pressure on children
by hurrying them through the process, and toward the product,
of becoming an adult. We, in effect, take childhood away from
our children.

In *The Hurried Child: Growing Up Too Fast Too Soon*, psychologist David Elkind warns:

> Hurried children are forced to take on the physical, psychologi-
> cal, and social trappings of adulthood before they are prepared to
> deal with them. We dress our children in miniature adult costumes
> (often with designer labels), we expose them to gratuitous sex and
> violence, and we expect them to cope with an increasingly be-
> wildering social environment—divorce, single parenthood, homo-
> sexuality. Through all these pressures the child senses that it is
> important for him or her to cope without admitting the confusion
> and pain that accompany such changes. Like adults, they are made
> to feel they must be survivors, and surviving means adjusting—
> even if the survivor is only four or six or eight years old. This
> pressure to cope without cracking is a stress in itself, the effects of
> which must be tallied with all the other effects of hurrying our
> children.[2]

For years, the "Barbie" doll has epitomized this phenomenon
to me. Barbie has a woman's sexually mature body. She is breast-
ed, small-waisted, leggy, and slender. Little girls are urged to
dress her up for her dates with "Ken," the accompanying male
doll. It is an altogether adolescent way of engaging in early

childhood play. It is vastly different from playing with baby dolls or stuffed animals. But most parents have literally bought into the Barbie doll marketing ploy over the last two decades. Because of it, little girls continue to fantasize that they are Barbie. Indeed, they look forward to the time when they can grow up and actually be like Barbie.

Television is another "hurrying" force in a child's life, and a formidable force it is. It is, in a sense, a new form of child abuse created by our enthusiasm for the technological age. Television permeates a child's life. Certainly it permeates my children's lives, and I expect it permeates yours too. Statistically, we cannot escape it. Television is a member of our families.

I know something of the influence television has. I produce and "star on" an educational children's television program and have done so for several years. I never cease to be amazed at how recognizable I am both to children and their parents in grocery stores and restaurants and other public places. I am a figure of awe to many of these children. I am told repeatedly by parents of the "power" I hold over their children. By this, they mean the power of persuasion. Just by virtue of being a "media personality," I can convince children of nearly anything I choose. Whatever I say, they will believe, and they believe me simply because I am on television. The "logic" behind this deference to my opinions seems to be something along the order of "if she didn't know what she was talking about, why would she be allowed to come into our living rooms?"

What's true and what's not is a perplexing issue to children—and to adults too. It is perplexing to adults because children aren't aware that they don't know the differences between reality and fantasy. They believe they have it "figured out." Our dilemma is how to show them that they haven't.

Since I appear on the same channel as other media personalities, children as old as nine or ten believe favorites like Michael Jackson and Mr. T are neighbors and friends of mine. They think I live in "Hollywood," wherever that mystical land is, and lead a very glamorous life that they would like to have too. But even those who know I live close to where they live have a ready image of me. One young friend of mine, five-year-old Nathan, once drove up to my house with his father and exclaimed in astonishment, "But, Dad, she doesn't live in a mansion!" Never doubt it, television is an exceedingly powerful medium. I don't think we have even begun to understand its impact on our children's lives.

One of the things that television programs do, as well as the commercials supporting them, is sweep away conceptual and logical impediments to comprehension. They allow free access to information and ideas that children would not have if they had to wait until they could read. Television removes intellectual barriers, extending sensory experiences in ways that were not possible before its advent into our homes. "Scenes of violence or of sexual intimacy that a young child could not conjure up from a verbal description are presented directly and graphically" on the TV screen, as Elkind reminds us.

Because urban women from ages eighteen to forty-five are the primary consumers of our country—or, in other words, because they buy more products than anyone else—television programming is geared toward what they will watch. Advertisers will not purchase commercial time unless they can be assured a large proportion of the eighteen-to-forty-five age-bracket will be in front of the program containing the advertising. Economics control the industry.

Even though my own educational show was number one in the ratings in its weekday format (appearing five mornings a week at 9:30), I was told its demographics were "wrong." Ironic as it may seem, "too many children" were watching it. While it was acknowledged that thousands of TVs were tuned-in to my show, no one could prove mothers were watching with their kids. The truth of it is, the advertisers seek the mothers, not the non-spending pre-eighteen-year-old children. Thus, my show was moved to early morning weekends (times normally dead for adult viewing) in order to make room for the more lucrative soaps and game shows on weekdays.

As Geoffrey Cowan has said, "If middle-aged or elderly peo-ple in a small town in rural America feel that television ignores their tastes and offers little that is nourishing to children, they are right."[3] We *all* watch, no matter what our interests, the types of shows that have mass appeal to the average person who is known to spend most of the family's income. Children are hurried toward adulthood in this significant fashion, and it can be unsettling and confusing, if not blatantly damaging.

Schools, too, take a role in this "hurrying" of children toward adulthood. Our schools have acquired an "assembly line" quali-ty. Children are seen as empty bottles waiting to be filled, with each grade making them fuller through each progression along the system. When they leave it—presto!—they are filled to the top, supposedly fully educated and ready to face the world (unless the bottle is defective, of course, in which case the "fillers" can't be responsible).

Because universal schooling was introduced as a way to pre-pare children for the industrialization of America, it is not sur-prising that schools have taken on this character. But factory work, as it used to be known, is now obsolete. Thus does Elkind say, "Our schools . . . are out of synch with the larger society and represent our past rather than our future." Certainly chil-dren caught in this outmoded information delivery system are astute enough to recognize the lag between what they are learn-ing in school and what is happening in the rest of the world.

Through irrelevancy to their lives, many students do poorly in school. Daniel Fader says it even stronger. "[Teachers] are worse than irrelevant," he writes in *The Naked Children,* "we are incoherent."[4] Yet making good grades and "succeeding" in school are rewarded by schools and society alike: honor lists are published and grade point averages have a great deal to do with getting into prestigious colleges or jobs. Knowing how to cope with this bewildering system is, not surprisingly, traumatic to many children. Worse than traumatic, many lose their way, and maybe their chance at a healthy life, in the confusing maze labeled "education."

But this is not all that is traumatic about the system. At least some school failure is attributable to the fear students and teachers have of being physically injured. (Parents fear for their children too.) We hear about "druggies" and gangs and other horror stories from public schools (though, I promise you, these tales aren't confined to any one type of environment). No matter where it occurs, physical abuse from peers, maybe even more than from adults, leads to high-level emotional stress.

Eddie, a seventh grade boy I know, was repeatedly taunted and beaten during his gym period by a band of thugs. But the teacher never seemed to be where he could see it happening. Eddie did not tell the teacher or anyone what he was enduring. He thought it was unmanly not to be able to handle it by himself. Yet neither did he ever hit back, for fear of getting in worse trouble. Thus, he found himself in a double bind, stymied as to how to protect himself and helpless to cope with the new terrors of his adolescent existence. Stoically he bore it all inside himself, though his fear of going to gym became a fear of going to school. Tension mounted. Every day Eddie hurt all through his head and his stomach. He could not concentrate on anything except surviving one more gym period. Coping with this single daily problem used up all of Eddie's emotional reserves. He had no mental energy left to give to his classwork. He stopped turning in assignments. In fact, he nearly flunked out of seventh grade.

Symptoms: Clues to What's Really Happening

It was at this point, with his near-failing grades on public record, that Eddie began to get some attention from adults. People began to ask, "What in the world are you doing, Eddie? You have to get those grades up. You have to get those missed assignments in. You can't keep on like this."

It was also the beginning of Eddie's loss of innocence, a loss which comes with discovering the terrible truth that the world is a frightening place where everyone, more or less, "goes it alone." Very little human protection is available to any of us. Eddie learned that if those stronger than he didn't "get" him for doing nothing (thugs beating him up in gym class), they would "get" him for doing something (making lousy grades). He saw no one willing to look at him for what was going on inside of him, no one who could see and recognize his feelings without first drawing attention to, and attempting to correct, his actions.

Eddie isn't alone in his quandary. My sixteen-year-old son, Marc, wrote the following sonnet, a poem he entitled "Sole Soul."

> Why doesn't anybody understand?
> Does anybody think the same as me?
> Are people just afraid to speak out free?
> I feel like a stranger in this land,
> A lonely grain in a vast beach of sand.
> I keep on looking but I cannot see
> The things society would have me be.
> I'm waiting for someone to take my hand.
>
> Continuously yearning for a love
> That deep down my heart fears I'll never find;
> And when I feel this I forget to try
> To please the most important One above.
> As I put on a mask to hide behind,
> Deep in my soul I silently cry.

Marc gave me permission to use his poem in this book, and I thank him very much for his willingness "to speak out free" on feelings he shares with other teens caught in his same predicament. Marc frequently feels alone with his feelings, but he is not. Though admission comes hard, other young people are just as confused about society's expectations for them as Marc is.

Marc also tells me that most adults who work with him are more concerned with what he does on the outside than what is happening to him on the inside, and I believe him. I have seen this communicated, whether inadvertently or not. They look at his achievements, at his grades and external behaviors, and then they judge him as being good or bad, worthy or not, based on criteria they have established. They look at the *what* of his life, rather than the *why*. Marc says that when he is conforming to adult expectations of him, all is right in the world of authority. But he does not see much evidence that it makes a difference to those in control whether all is right with *his* world or not. Instead, the point seems to be, how well is he adapting to *theirs*?

In his poem, Marc speaks of putting on "a mask to hide behind." He is convinced adults like him better with his mask on. He believes he makes them uncomfortable when he takes it off. Marc, to *my* mind, is simply one of the most charming, delightful young men I have ever had the privilege of knowing. That this kind of intelligent, astute sensitivity resides in my house is, I know, a gift sent directly from God to make me into a better human being. And because Marc has the ability to express himself, he becomes a voice for those who are less articulate than he.

Thomas Cottle tells of Bobby, a young man not unlike Marc. "No one likes to recognize what people like me have to go through," Bobby says. "I'm sure if you asked most people they'd say the life of a teenager is a dream. Everyone I talk to seems to want to be young again, which is one of the sicknesses of the culture. . . . Teenagers, or whatever you want to call us, are people. Real, live people."[5]

Real, live people express themselves in all sorts of ways. Sometimes, if the message is as real as the person sending it, we are not comfortable receiving it. We are not comfortable because it frequently is telling us something we would rather not hear. Authors Paul Ackerman and Murray Kappelman call these messages "signals." Signals are like harbingers, or message-bearers.

When we're ill, we are more knowledgeable about our symptoms than we are the cause of our disease. We go to a doctor to learn that. We want help to get at the root of what's wrong with us. What good is treatment of the symptoms if no one is trying to cure the disease? Concentrating on outer symptoms and ignoring their inner origin is not any more satisfactory for schools than it is for medicine.

Thinking of signals from children in this way brings us to a basic tenet of communication: communication requires not only a sender but a receiver. The signals being sent by troubled youngsters, according to Ackerman and Kappelman, are things like temper tantrums, fantasy friends, lying and stealing, bed-wetting and soiling, stuttering, hyperactivity, shyness and with-drawal, running away from home, refusal to eat, sleeplessness, sibling rivalry, immature behavior, school phobia, failing in school, overreaction, friendlessness, excessive attachment, fre-quent physical complaints, antisocial behavior, male effeminate and female masculine behaviors, suicide threats, and promis-cuity.[6] Our job is to *receive* the signals, not as ends in them-selves, but as clues to the larger picture of what is actually distressing the child. We must put the pieces together and find out what is *really being said to us*.

Remember Eddie and his infamous gym class? Eddie was waiting for someone to put the pieces together. Someone had to "read" the signal of his failing grades as more than "just a dumb kid who needs to turn his work in." Lack of intelligence or not turning his work in weren't either of Eddie's problems. And if he did turn the work in and improved his grades, so what? How was that going to solve Eddie's authentic problem, his difficul-ties with the gang in gym class and the consequent blows to his self-esteem? He needed a caring adult to get at the *why* behind his behavior, and not one who was concerned, instead, with just correcting the *what*.

Visualizing Prayer: Power and the Imagination

"There is not a living soul who has no spiritual understand-ing," wrote the late Agnes Sanford in her book *The Healing Light*. "If the spirit does not respond to us, it may be because we have not sufficient love and sympathy to forget ourselves and look into the being of the one whom we must help."[7]

It is the duty of every Christian to pray for everyone. Christian teachers *must* pray for their students. Christians working in schools should pray for the professional staff, as well as the children who are in the building. But only the Holy Spirit can direct the healing power of our prayers. And if we will listen to the voice of God within us (and we must become wise as to how he communicates), we will be led to those who need even more specific prayers. Agnes Sanford tells us that "the impulse of love" is the voice of God within, and we should never be afraid to follow that impulse's leading. But it is not only unnecessary to say, "God told me to pray for you," it is unwise. The sound of piousness never facilitates healing.

Many, many of today's children need emotional healing even more than they need physical healing. And it is a healing of their memories that is the most critical ingredient for their emotional well-being.

Bill Vaswig knows what healing of memories is all about. Bill, a successful church pastor, prayed daily but did not know the joy of "getting through." When his eldest son had to undergo psychiatric treatment for schizophrenia, Bill's prayers seemed to bounce off the ceiling and not go anywhere.

In his dramatic book, *I Prayed, He Answered,* he tells of approaching a diminutive woman named Agnes Sanford, and through the power of visualizing prayer that she taught him, seeing his son completely healed. "I came to understand that my words are but the smallest part of prayer," Bill says today. As Bill Vaswig learned, God touches us and the people we pray for through our imaginations:

> Many times I have prayed for children who disturb classrooms, and they respond rapidly. Most children who constantly harass teachers do not need spankings. They probably have already had enough of those. They need someone to take them on their lap and pray for them.
>
> Usually I pray that God will cause the little child to see himself as accepted and as a worthwhile person. If praying for a little boy, I often ask him if he ever hit a home run or more than a single. If he

says yes, I ask him if he remembers how happy his teammates were. Usually he remembers very well. So I ask the boy to picture himself rounding third base with all his friends cheering him on and loving him.

Then in my prayer, I ask God to quiet down the little storm within him and help him see himself as a loved, neat kid. Almost without exception such prayers help the child very much. Since it is easy to get back into old patterns of behavior, I may pray for the child again within a week and then in two weeks and again after a month.[8]

Once, as I sat in an audience listening to Bill Vaswig speak, I became a little girl again. Bill "regressed" us not through hypnotism but through prayer. He led his audience's imaginations gently around the labyrinth of our adult years and back to a time when, as young children five years old, we were each to be sitting in a chair—our favorite chair—in our family living room.

I pictured my chair perfectly in my mind. It was a big overstuffed chair encased in a faded, floral-print, cotton slipcover. Its arms would have been wide enough for me to sit on, but I had slid all the way to the back of the broad seat itself, my short legs straight out with knees locked, my toes in white socks and small brown oxfords pointing up to the ceiling. I was bent over a Sears & Roebuck Christmas catalog, my eyes intent and lips slightly parted, my hair held back on the side by a blue plastic barrette which appeared to be in the shape of a Mexican sombrero. I have no idea where the image came from, but it was vivid and real. I *saw* myself as I had been, in surroundings containing exact details which should have long been forgotten (in subsequent conversations, my amazed mother has confirmed what I "saw").

As I sat in that auditorium, caught in my first personal experience with the power of visualizing prayer, Bill Vaswig helped me hear a knock on my front door. No one else was at home, so I set down my catalog (left open to the page I had been looking at), scooted forward to get my small frame out of the deep chair, and went to answer the knock. Jesus was at the door, but he didn't look as I expected him to look. Still, I knew it was Jesus. He had the nicest eyes I'd ever seen. He picked me up in his arms and held me against him. I was totally unafraid. And he said, with great warmth and conviction, separating each word for emphasis, "I love you." I could feel his beard, and I could smell his scent, and the strength of his love washed all through me.

In my seat in the filled auditorium, against anything I could do to stop it, I began quietly to weep. It was an actual physical sensation. I was jolted. Though I had been a long-time Christian, I'd felt nothing like it before. It was release and it was joy and it was awe and amazement. I knew Jesus loved me. I positively *knew* it.

And he said to me, "Aren't you going to invite me in?" So, of course, I did, and I took him on a journey throughout my house (the house I actually lived in at age five), and I showed him the kitchen and the table in the alcove where we all ate and which seat was mine and which ones were everyone else's. I took him upstairs and pointed out the single bed where I slept and, next to it, the one where my sister slept. At the end of the hall, I showed him where my parents' room was. Though I also have a brother, I did not show Jesus where my brother slept. My brother was not born until I was six, and without even giving it conscious thought, I excluded in my imagination what would have been impossible for me to know at age five.

Jesus was interested in everything he saw, in everything I showed and told him. I took him back down to the living room, and we rested together in the fat floral-patterned chair I had been in earlier (there was room in it for both of us), and we began looking at the catalog I'd put down. I pointed out each item I wanted for Christmas, and Jesus was interested in that too.

Throughout this episode I knew such complete and accepting love that I was able to progress forward mentally through the terrors of childhood and the insecurities of adolescence, safely

surrounded by the power of Christ. It was an amazing experience, and it was a start toward the healing of some of my own
hurtful, post-five-year-old memories. The bad things couldn't
touch me, not really, because Christ's love was there to protect
me as I "grew back" to my present age.

I doubt I have done a very adequate job of describing what
really happened to me that day in Bill Vaswig's audience. Having been raised in a very orthodox, fairly nondemonstrative and
certainly nonverbal Christian environment, there was nothing
like this visual imagining in my prayer life or in any of my prior
religious experiences. Theologically, I do not consider myself a
"radical" or a "kook." In fact, though I am not proud to admit it,
I have even been vocally intolerant of those I feared might be.
But this phenomenon began to make me a believer in the
positive power of the imagination as nothing else has.

Healing from a Distance: Prayer in Classrooms

We have been talking so far about prayer experiences that
more or less enlist the cooperation of the person being prayed
for. This, of course, is impossible in public school classrooms
where separation of church and state exists. Fortunately, active
cooperation is not necessary for visualizing prayer to work.

Agnes Sanford calls the capacity for this type of prayer "healing from a distance." The first step in achieving the power to
heal from a distance is to recognize that there is only one in all
the world who dwelt perfectly in God and yet remained firmly
in the flesh, and that is the man Jesus Christ. He is our intercessor, our brother in prayer. Agnes tells us how to ready ourselves for the Christ-infusion experience:

> In order to fill ourselves with His whole being, let us think of
> Him, imagining His presence, seeing Him with the eyes of the mind,
> trying to love Him with the heart. Let us beseech Him to come and
> dwell within us. Let us ask Him to enter into our spirits and fill us
> with His own consciousness of the fatherhood of God; to enter into

our minds and think within us His own thoughts; to enter into our hearts and feel through us His own love, directing it to those who need it most; to enter into our bodies and build them up according to the pattern of His perfect holiness, making us more and more fit channels for the inflow and outflow of His life.[9]

"Seeing with the eyes of the mind"—our imaginations are greatly underrated! While words can fail us, the power of the mind cannot. Indeed, most of its potential, all those complex interconnections between the billions of neurons that God placed in our heads, remains untapped. During a lifetime there can be stored in our brain ten times more information than all that is contained in the volumes of the Library of Congress. Nine-tenths of our thoughts lie below the conscious level, with perhaps only one impulse in a million reaching beyond the spinal cord into the upper levels of the brain. The forces of spirit, mind, and body are synchronized and ordered by the same inner control center, and that which affects one affects the others. Positivism affects positively; negativism affects negatively.

Agnes Sanford defines Christianity as "reaching the white light of the creator God, finding the human loveliness of Jesus Christ, and by the power of the Holy Spirit re-creating man in the image of Christ through seeing Christ in man." She also maintains that doing this in prayer is so simple that any child can learn it. It is merely to connect in spirit with the love of God, send that love to another person, and see him or her re-created in goodness and joy and peace. This, then, is the crux of visualizing prayer which can, indeed, heal from a distance. Agnes Sanford quotes a child to whom she taught this technique:

> "Wow! I never saw anything work like that in my life! Before I got up this morning, I lay there and thought of my Mom like she is when she's all happy, and I said, 'Thank you, God, because you love her and you're making her like that now.' And then I thought that way about my Dad, too. And my Mom, she came up and kissed me and she smiled so nice I just stood there and looked at her! And my

Dad, he pulled out [some money] and said, 'Here, go and have a good time, Kid.' Wow! I never saw anything like that in my life!"[10]

Several years ago my son was having a very difficult time adjusting to first grade. He would hide so that no one could find him when it was time to go to school. He was moody and dour, a quite visibly unhappy young man. His temper took on startling proportions. Until he exhibited it, I really had not been aware that a six-year-old was capable of such consuming rage.

One night, in a small prayer support group that met at our home on Sunday evenings, we shared our concern about our young son. We all prayed for him, and as we prayed, we held the image of him as the smiling, happy child he used to be in our minds. As he slept down the hall from where we prayed, we imagined him being surrounded in his bed by God's protective light. Nothing could get through it that God didn't allow to get through. We "saw" him waking up, loving again and laughing again, a normal, healthy first grader. The next morning, we encountered no less than a miracle. When God answers prayer, he truly does so in abundance.

This child, who to this day still does not rise from his pillow without overt coercion, shouted, "Good morning!" exuberantly from his top bunk. And those words were, amazingly, followed by, "I love you, Mom! I love you, Dad! What's for breakfast?"

His teacher called later that week to exclaim about the change in him. To what, she wanted to know, did we attribute it? "God," we said, sending another silent prayer of gratitude heavenward. Through visualizing prayer, we had been able to see our son as we knew God wanted him. "So be it" was all that remained to make it happen.

Imagine the power this unleashes for the Christian teacher in the classroom! Obviously, it unleashes it in the home. Indeed, it unleashes prayer-power everywhere.

On one of Agnes Sanford's most joyful days (which were, she

said, her "most powerful days"), she entered the elevator of a tall building with a dejected, sagging-looking woman.

"I bless you in the name of the Lord," Agnes thought as they rode upward together. "I see you as a child of God, strong and refreshed and joyful, for through my prayers His strength is entering into you."

The women's bent shoulders lifted immediately, and when she alighted from the elevator, she went confidently down the corridor, her head held high.

When we hear stories like this we are continually amazed and delighted that God loves us and listens to us, that the "guiding Intelligence of the universe really cares for our small concerns." We may be skeptical, of course, until such experiences happen to us. But that's why we need to be "risking" so that such experiences *will* happen, and thus, teach us. By "daring to try God and see whether His promises are true," as Agnes Sanford challenged, we will discover a lavishness of love which overwhelms.

According to author Bruce Larson, wholeness cannot be achieved without risking danger. I have found this to be true. Once, in a powerful moment of daring to draw near to God, with my husband's impetus and prayer intervention, I surrendered to Christ a load of guilt I had been carrying for years. Jesus took the heaviness from me immediately, and I actually felt his inflowing forgiveness. It was warm, and I was light. Fred's arms were around me tightly, and he felt it too. Through his love for me, Fred was able to know the same sense of release I knew. It is the only time I recall seeing him give himself over to tears of joy. Unashamed, we wept together.

While I can now think back on the causes of the guilt, there is no pain in the memory. The guilt weighting me down was lifted, and when it's lifted by Christ, he never gives it back. He carries it forever. My experience was not with long distance prayer per se (sometimes beneficiaries of long-distance prayer are ignorant of it; thus, it is difficult to testify to it from the receiving end), but my experience does proclaim the *long-term* effects—indeed, the staying power—of intercessory prayer.

Just as nothing is too great for Christ, neither is anything too small. By visualizing her children as happy and at peace (as she knew God intended them to be), by constantly holding the image of their smiling, healthy faces in her mind and saying, "Thank you, God, for making it so," Agnes Sanford provided what her children laughingly called *discipline by remote control.* "Mom's up to her tricks again," they would say when the evidence of her prayers filled their consciousness. God responded to Agnes Sanford, knowing from whom her faith to command came. She had learned how to make the connection with him.

Visualizing prayer is simple and strong. It is the way to keep our prayers from bouncing off the ceiling and going nowhere. Bill Vaswig was told, "You preachers know everything about praying except how to make it work." It was a statement that haunted him for years, because he feared it was true. His friend Agnes Sanford, commissioned by God, helped change all that for him. We, too, are commissioned by God, and there are children waiting for us to help change things for them as well.

Therapeutic Schools: Achieving Emotional Wholeness

In *Children without Childhood,* an observant study conducted in the early 1980s, Marie Winn comments that "something has happened to the joys of childhood." And we can see that she's right. After inspecting the many societal reasons for the changes, Winn goes on to challenge us: "Can the boundaries between adulthood and childhood be once again restored? Can parents today, who sense uneasily that something is missing, try to re-create a different sort of childhood that they themselves once enjoyed? In an Age of Preparation, can individual parents hope to buck the tide and try to bring their children up protectively?"[11]

Child development experts have warned that the early

years—the preschool years—are crucial to later adult intellectual and mental health. Indeed, they have warned of it so
strongly that our society has reacted just as strongly to their
advice. Through our actions, it would seem we have determined
that if these are the "most important" years, nothing else beyond them must matter much. We tend to believe we have
"set" our children on a lifetime course before age five. Guilt
consumes us if we fear we've failed our children in their early
years; complacency prevails if we feel we haven't. Either way,
we tend to give up most of our nurturing opportunities during
our children's middle childhood and adolescent years.

But as child development specialist Dr. Annie Herman postulates, those early childhood years, while forming a basic personality, may not necessarily be the most crucial ones. "There is a
certain resilience in early childhood," she explains to Marie
Winn, "but this resilience slowly disappears. When you are
resilient you bounce back. Thus young children can recover
from physical and mental trauma quickly and put things aside
and turn to other things. But as they grow older their resilience
is diminished. At this point the child becomes far more vulnerable to outside experience. Now the child can suffer permanent
damage."[12]

To understand why contemporary youngsters are exhibiting
signs of more trauma than in years past, let us examine the basic
difference between today's children and yesterday's children.
Today, school-age children, through changes in family stability
and the proliferation of television, are burdened early with
adult pressures, responsibilities, and knowledge. Youngsters of
the past (even those growing up a mere fifteen years ago) knew
that children were children and adults were adults and that,
despite the wretchedness they might occasionally glimpse in the
adult world, they could still remain, in their different state,
untouched by it.

In *Growing Up*, journalist Russell Baker describes his own
childhood during the Depression years, a childhood which was
darkened by poverty, marital discord, illness, and death. But he

says: "The occasional outbursts of passion that flickered across my childhood were like summer storms. The sky clouded sud-denly, thunder rumbled, lightning flashed and I trembled a few moments, then just as swiftly the sky turned blue again and I was basking contentedly again in the peace of innocence."[13] It was not the complete absence of unhappiness that allowed Rus-sell Baker to look back on his childhood as an island of peace and innocence. It was that he was allowed the simple pleasures of growing up—of play, imagination, curiosity, and the pursuit of adventure—and was not pulled into partnership with adult miseries. Such a conjunction would have been unthinkable.

We cannot reverse the societal changes that have gotten us here. We cannot, in Marie Winn's words, "return to the old-style family with the bread-earning father and the childlike, stay-at-home mother minding the house and kids." Indeed, it is questionable whether such a step backward in time is desirable.

To expect the women's movement, which brought a new maturity to femininity, to call for a reinstatement of female dependency and lack of career options is unrealistic. Women need the opportunity to fulfill their God-given potential. Christ, the first great women's liberator, admonished Martha to leave her "duties" in the kitchen so she could, instead, seek the same priorities for her life as her sister Mary had found (Luke 10:39–42).

Neither can we expect the dominant part that television plays in children's lives to disappear. If we ban television from our own homes, our children will be exposed to it in their friends' homes. Besides, television *can,* through responsible management, be a positive influence. At its best, it is both enlightening and entertaining.

The children most in need of healing and most vulnerable to the hurts of their world are those of school-age. This fact has a major impact on what should be happening in schools. *These* are the children who are growing up like burned-out adults en-trapped in a mid-life crisis. It is the students in elementary and secondary classrooms who are most subject to permanent emotional damage. They are the age-group to whom our concern must specifically be directed. Thus, schools need to provide not only an academic environment (which we will explore more in the next two chapters) but a therapeutic environment as well.

Classrooms, in order to be therapeutic, must not take their signals from society's contradictions but from psychology's implications. In *The Psychology of Jesus and Mental Health,* Raymond Cramer cites the sixth beatitude, "Happy are the pure in heart; they will see God" (Matt. 5:8, TEV), as providing the key to attitude reconstruction. But to the average reader, the sixth beatitude is frightening. We know we are *not* pure in heart. Therefore, we fear for our capability of ever seeing God. Seeing God, however, is a promise so great that all other promises pale in comparison. Don't we owe it to ourselves to try to explore how to attain it?

Cramer goes on to show us that the word "pure" appears twenty-eight times in the New Testament. At least ten of those times, it can be translated "clean." The other eighteen times it means "clear." In fact, the word "pure" as it appears in the sixth beatitude is derived from the Greek word *katharizō,* meaning "to cleanse or make pure." As a psychological term, "catharsis" signifies the discharge of repressed ideas or emotions, while in medical terminology the Greek word *katharsis* has reference to a purgative—a cathartic which cleanses or purges.[14] Happy are those who are healed of their pent-up hurts . . . for they shall see God.

We cannot see God until we feel his impact in our innermost being. If our emotions are not balanced, we cannot see God because our vision of him will be "distorted, warped and twisted." *Our very concept of God depends on the condition of our hearts and minds.* Of such is the necessity for attitude reconstruction born. In the psychology of Jesus this means getting at the center of the problem—at the heart, or the inner person, where the change must take place.

"[We] must change the individual within before a re-education of his outward actions can take place," Cramer writes. "It is a psychological fact that if the mind is preconditioned along a certain line it will eventually have a tendency to inhibit or reject any thought which is different from the preconditioning. If only negative thoughts are constantly planted, no positive thoughts will be able to gain entrance."[15]

How often do teachers face students with average or above average ability who are unable to utilize their potential because they cannot manage their emotions or feelings? How often do *students* face *teachers* struggling against the same hindrance? "In my opinion," Cramer emphatically states, "the most important thing about us happens to lie in the area of our emotional responses."

Emotional hurts restrict God's entry into lives. Jesus admonished us to do nothing to spark these emotional hurts in children. "If anyone should cause one of these little ones to lose his faith in me, it would be better for that person to have a large millstone tied around his neck and be thrown into the sea" (Mark 9:42, TEV). This is a stern call for protectiveness.

We started out this section by looking at a challenge Marie Winn poses: Can we buck the tide of modern society and hope to bring up children protectively? The answer is: Yes. If Jesus requires it of us, he will provide the resources to make it occur.

But where to begin bucking the tide is a separate consideration. We need a beginning place. The beginning place for many hurt children is in the public schools. That is where the hope that something might be different for them first becomes a possibility. And just because we live under a constitutional arrangement demanding separation of church and state is no reason to despair. Christians can make a difference anyway. In fact, constitutional requirements have little impact when compared to the impact of God. And being "for or against prayer in schools" has nothing to do with it.

In order for the power of visualizing prayer to be unleashed, the pray-er needn't be demonstrative (in fact, it is better not to be), and the pray-er needn't enlist participation from the person being prayed for. The ability to pray through the "mind's eye" is the place to begin answering Dante Rossetti's question:

> What shall assuage the unforgotten pain
> And teach the unforgetful to forget?

We unleash God's power into students' lives by doing as Betsy's high school speech teacher did. Betsy was a victim of emotional abuse. For years, she had been called stupid and inept by relatives and teachers alike. Her high school speech teacher, however, wasn't having any part of those assessments. He believed in Betsy and was determined to make her believe in herself.

He urged her into preparing for the state competition in extemporaneous speaking, something Betsy had never done before. She felt inadequate and afraid. Indeed, the task seemed tremendous: keeping abreast of all current events by reading at least three news magazines weekly and a newspaper daily, by watching the national and international news on television nightly, and by keeping copious notes covering it all. Then, on the date of competition, the extemporaneous speaker would draw three topics, choose one, and be given thirty minutes to prepare a seven-minute speech. Betsy didn't want any part of it.

But this teacher was not moved by his student's insecurities. He told Betsy flatly, "If anyone can get a '1' rating in state, you can."

Grudgingly and timidly, Betsy set at the task. Before long, however, she was totally immersed in the project. Each day she was required to prepare a practice speech and give it to her teacher. He critiqued her, and sometimes he did not seem particularly kind in his comments. At those times, Betsy had to reach deeper inside herself. All the while, though, the teacher was praying for Betsy's willingness and future achievement. His prayers always included the visual image of Betsy standing up, strong and confident, delivering a first-class speech that would restore her faith in her abilities. Knowing that it was in God's will for Betsy to be emotionally whole, he would end each prayer with the words, "Thank you, God, for making it so."

Betsy picks up the story from here. "When the day of the speech festival arrived, I was not even nervous. I knew I could do it, and I wanted to do it—not only because of the work I had put into it, but for the work, time, and effort my speech teacher had given, too." She received a "1" rating in the state for extemporaneous speaking, but it was the least of the two gifts she was given that day.

Teaching can be perceived both as presenting a human invitation to learn subject matter and as presenting God's invitation to learn about ourselves and about him. Understanding the need for emotional wholeness is at the heart of teaching. Where there is a fracturing of the emotional spirit, healing must occur. Without it, nothing else can happen in the classroom. Learning is blocked by emotional obstructions.

In *Motivation and Personality,* Abraham Maslow pointed out the marked impact we all have on each other:

> Let people realize clearly that every time they threaten or humiliate or hurt unnecessarily or dominate or reject another human being, they become forces for the creation of psychopathology, even if these be small forces. Let them recognize that everyone who is kind, helpful, decent, psychologically democratic, affectionate, and warm is a psychotherapeutic force, even though a small one.[16]

Smallness doesn't matter. The effort to heal does.

CHAPTER FOUR

How Is It Possible to Learn
All This Stuff?

THE NEED FOR ENABLERS

*The best teacher is the one who, through
establishing a personal relationship, frees
the student to learn. Learning can only take
place in the student, and the teacher can only
create the conditions for learning.*

—C. H. Patterson—

Of his role in *The Natural,* an Arthurian-heroic film set in the
mystical world of baseball in the thirties, actor Robert Redford
observed simply, "Everybody in life wants his time at bat."

Lana was a child sent up to bat with two outs and a full count
against her. In third grade, like most children, Lana attempted
to master cursive writing. Her efforts did not conclude happily,
and to this day (Lana is now twenty-two) she is self-conscious
about her handwriting. A teacher informed Lana at eight years
old that her handwriting gave people the impression she was not
very intelligent. While the teacher's intent may have been to
motivate Lana to improve, it is not the sort of enabling any child
needs. Instead, because of poor "umpiring," Lana was actually
disabled. Calling a ball a strike, as any fan knows, doesn't make
it so. But Lana was too young to argue with the ump's call. She
accepted it, not seeing that sometimes even teachers are wrong.

On the other hand, Lenny was fortunate enough to be enabled. At least, he was enabled for a time. With the classification of "learning disabled" securely intact, Lenny reached the third grade as a distinct behavior problem. He knew the label attached to him, and his response to it manifested itself in misbehavior. He was targeted by teachers for the "personal-social adjustment" class. The staffing (a meeting in which the professional staff sits down in a round-table discussion and determines a child's educational fate) was scheduled for February.

In January, Rachel walked into Lenny's life. Rachel was Lenny's new teacher. A December graduate just out of college, Rachel was a beginning teacher, and Lenny's class was her first. Like many beginning teachers, she was positive and idealistic. But Rachel had more going for her than sunny idealism. She was also a Christian.

Rachel knew little about staffings, but she knew enough about the "PSA" program to know Lenny was going to have a hard time in later life recovering from his consignment there. She didn't want him to go, though neither did she particularly want a severe behavior disruption in her class. Still, when all was said and done, Lenny's needs took precedence over her needs. This Rachel adamantly believed.

Before the staffing, one experienced teacher—who would be getting Lenny in fourth grade if he wasn't moved into the personal-social adjustment track—took Rachel aside. "Now, watch what you say," this teacher said quietly to Rachel. "If we play our cards right, we'll get this problem [meaning Lenny] out of our hair."

Rachel was incensed, and her resolve not to let Lenny go became strengthened. She fought for Lenny in that staffing. One of her astonished colleagues said with a measure of accuracy, "You don't know Lenny like we do. You just got here."

"But that's just the point," protested Rachel just as accurately. "I haven't had a chance to work with him. Please let me have that chance before you send him to PSA. Let me try. Isn't this too serious not to let me at least try?"

So Lenny, or Rachel, or both, got a chance "at bat." And through the next weeks Lenny responded to Rachel's belief in him. He would finish work, even though it was often a simpler assignment than what his peers were working on. Still, it was the first time he had ever finished work of any kind. He began to smile again. He even took correction from Rachel without a display of temper. She offered discipline sternly, no punches pulled, but she offered it in love, and Lenny knew that. He calmed down under her tutelage. There had been a need inside of him to prove himself, although he had also needed the right set of circumstances to bring it about. Rachel had provided the atmosphere he required. As May approached, and the fourth grade teacher's dread of getting Lenny became palpable, Rachel, with a note of sorrowful desperation, asked me, "What's going to happen to Lenny now?"

Cultural Norms: A Traditional View of Schooling

How Lana or Lenny or any student *felt* about their experience in classrooms or with teachers has not historically been of much interest to schools. Feelings, or affective concerns, were not part of a teacher's instructional objectives in the early days of formal education. If feelings mattered at all, they did so in the context of turning personal alienation into a reflection of the work ethic—dedication to the idea of work itself.

In the first part of the twentieth century, industrialists and some school officials were worried about finding workers who would be content to work at boring and repetitive tasks. This was the type of laborer that the Industrial Age required. As Daniel Selakovich writes in *Schooling in America,* "The schools were called upon to train such workers not only in the minimal skills needed to man the machines but, more importantly, in the right attitudes which would make them happy with their work."[1] The ordinary virtues of devotion, loyalty, and obedience were extolled as important to the preservation and progress of the democratic ideal. "The perfect society was

comprised of workers who were happy in their menial tasks—
productive, obedient, and law-abiding citizens."

Even Eleanor Roosevelt tacitly added her stamp of approval
to this basic premise in a foreword to *Talks with Teachers*.
"From the start teachers must realize that they are shaping
human beings who must eventually be the kind of people who
will be good citizens of a democracy," Mrs. Roosevelt wrote.
"That was the whole objective of our forefathers in starting
public education in our country."[2]

Our own parents' attitudes taught that you went to your job
daily, year after year, and, if you wanted additional fulfillment,
you came home to your hobbies. Personal satisfaction and working twenty or thirty years for the same employer had little or no
relation to each other, except as the latter defined the former
through achieving the cultural equivalent of a "gold watch."
Only with the current generation of young professionals do we
note any substantial shift from this attitude.

Those commonly held values of loyalty and commitment to a
single task have long been associated with the democratic mission of the public school. As early as 1852 the notion that the
school could provide an effective training ground for factory
workers was expressed by the Lowell, Massachusetts, school
"board." The reign of big industry in our country, and its con-
tiguous reign in public schooling, ran unchecked throughout the
two twenty-five year periods on either side of 1900. Democratic
education meant a school system that supported the existing
political, social, and—especially—economic systems. While
the nature of work has significantly changed since that time, the
nature of schools has not kept pace with the changes.

Many scholars have studied the history of schools in the
United States and reached the conclusion that schools have
never promoted the democratic ideal. These scholars see schools
as having promoted narrow and selfish class interests which,
instead, have made them instrumental in conserving what is
basically an undemocratic and limited system.

Colin Greer, in *The Great School Legend,* concluded that

schools not only failed in their democratic promise but served as
a major obstacle to the realization of the ideals of equality and
economic and social justice. It was a myth that schools took
children of the poor and immigrants and minorities from their
conditions of ignorance and poverty and elevated them into the
mainstream of society. According to Greer, "the failure of many
children has been, and still is, a learning experience precisely
appropriate to the place assigned them and their families in the
social order. They are being taught to fail and to accept their
failure."[3]

Perhaps Richard Hofstadter was right when he declared that
the kindest thing one could find to say about public schooling
was that it "was meant to take a vast, heterogeneous, and
mobile population . . . and forge it into a nation, make it literate, and give it . . . the minimal civic competence necessary to
the operation of republican institutions."[4]

At any rate, one fact remains irrevocably clear: the teacher as
a dispenser of information and the student as a receptacle to be
filled according to the teacher's purposes (which generally reflect those of society's) continues today as the most popular
mode of classroom interaction. One of my university counter-
parts goes so far as to assert that he considers he has taught
whether anyone has learned or not. Transmitting learning is not
his responsibility; teaching is. He views them as mutually exclusive acts. Furthermore, he says that if he "practices" his
lecture in front of an empty classroom, then delivers it again in
front of a full classroom, he has taught not once but twice. In
any case, learning is not the point.

This supposition brings to the surface an old debate in educational circles over whether teaching is a science or whether it is
an art. Proponents for teaching as a science argue for increasing
teacher awareness of specific methodologies and systems. What
works in one case will work in another. It is like a doctor
knowing which medication will counteract which disease. In
the scientific view of teaching, the teacher diagnoses student
difficulties and follows a set of prescriptions to correct them.

The medical profession and teaching are seen by many as being analogous activities.

Proponents for teaching as an art, on the other hand, point out the wide diversity among people. Not everyone responds the same way to a given stimulus, so there is an unpredictable quality to classroom life. No single methodology will work at all times and in all cases. Students have different learning styles, for one thing. Teaching becomes a judgment call, bringing together various characteristics of student individuality with appropriate instructional methods the teacher always has ready and available in an internalized "knapsack of ideas." Teacher knowledge of specific methodologies and prescriptions becomes important only in the sense that the more a teacher knows, the more possible applications there can be for individual situations.

What all of this means to our study of the need for enablers is that there is a congruent need to know what imparting knowledge is. How is someone to enable learning if operating under a distorted view of teaching? What, then, *will* become of Lenny?

Imparting Knowledge: Disinviting vs. Inviting

William Watson Purkey has long been associated with the concept of invitational teaching. With the collaboration of John Novak, Purkey has published a new edition of his *Inviting School Success: A Self-Concept Approach to Teaching and Learning*. It contains an eminently readable and commonsensical analysis of what actually goes on when students learn and when they fail to learn. Christians, whether graduates of teacher training programs or not, have enormous opportunity to "teach" under the Purkey/Novak system:

> Everyone and everything in schools should invite the realization of human potential. This involves the *people* (teachers, bus drivers, aides, cafeteria staff, secretaries, librarians, nurses, counselors, custodians, crossing guards, administrators), the *places* (classrooms, offices, hallways, commons, restrooms, playing fields, gymnasiums,

libraries), the *policies* (rules, codes, procedures), and the *programs* (curricular or extracurricular). Everybody and everything can and should invite students to develop intellectually, socially, psychologically, and physically. We call this entire process *invitational education.*[5]

What we have here is a more dynamic concept of teaching and learning than was ever thought of by those involved in transmitting the cultural norms of society throughout education's history. Over and over, we see a teacher's attitudes toward her or his students as either helping or hindering those students toward a belief that they can learn—with "teacher" being defined as anybody who plays an essential role in the education of children.

In their book, Purkey and Novak go on to discuss four levels, from disinviting to inviting, at which individuals in schools conceivably could function. It is important to note, these authors tell us, that "what is attractive or repellent remains in the eyes of the beholder." No matter how good intentions are, if behaviors are not viewed positively by others, they do not issue invitations.

The four categories of behaviors are: intentionally disinviting, unintentionally disinviting, unintentionally inviting, and intentionally inviting. Pay special attention to the modifiers affecting the "disinviting" and "inviting" aspects, because through them is revealed the heart of invitational teaching. The results of disinviting, whether unintentional or intentional, are the same; the results of inviting, whether unintentional or intentional, are also the same. And student perception, not teacher intention, renders a final judgment on which is a disinviting and which is an inviting act.

The disadvantage to both types of disinviting behavior is obvious. In either case, students are not enabled to learn. But the advantage to functioning at the *intentionally* inviting level as opposed to the *unintentionally* inviting level is that, in the first, educators consciously realize what is creating positive responses in their students. Unintentionally inviting teachers may bring about a positive response one day, but never be able to reestablish it. They cannot get it back because they remain ignorant of what caused it in the first place. On the other hand, Purkey and Novak call these operating at the highest level "artfully inviting" teachers. They "think in a special language of 'doing with' rather than 'doing to.'" They purposefully and deliberately behave in ways that invite students to get involved in their own education, that enable students to *learn*.

Teachers are no longer the focus of classrooms; students are. In this view of how to impart knowledge, teachers are simply, but very importantly, the instruments for learning, the causative agents for the development of important insights and concepts. Teachers set the stage where learning can play out its part inside of a student's head. Students are no longer seen as empty vessels needing filling. They are, instead, viewed as God's repositories. What they need is someone to help them understand what they already, through God's grace, contain within themselves. And among those things they contain is a vast and insatiable curiosity to learn and to know—as well as the urge to satisfy that curiosity.

Teachers can squelch the innate curiosity of their students, or they can call it forth. It is in incubation. We must provide the warm, lamp-like environment conducive to its full maturation. "Do not use harmful words, but only helpful words, the kind that build up and provide what is needed, so that what you say will do good to those who hear you" (Eph. 4:29, TEV).

Christ: God's Enabler

In *The Tempest*, Shakespeare cries in torment:

> You taught me language; and my profit on't
> Is, I know how to curse: the red plague rid you,
> For learning me your language!

And H. H. Munro, writing under his *nom de plume*, "Saki," declares in "The Baker's Dozen":

But, good gracious, you've got to educate him first. You can't expect a boy to be vicious till he's been to a good school.

The world was going to a "school" filled with cursing and viciousness until Christ entered it. The man Jesus Christ, Son of God, changed all that. At the very least, by changing it for us, he showed us how to change it for others.

If we are to speak of teaching as enabling, then we must recognize the greatest Enabler of all time. Through Christ, God enabled us to learn about his kingdom. Enabling is an action which facilitates, or makes easier, someone else's learning. God facilitated our learning about him by providing us with Jesus. For Christians, the qualities of enabling exemplified by Jesus are eminently important to a study of teaching and learning.

One reason that God sent us Christ was to make it easier for us to learn about his kingdom. Christ was the vehicle for putting God's kingdom into "simpler" or more easily understandable— fully human—terms. That doesn't mean that all who were intended to receive the message actually "got" it, of course. However, the fact that not everyone learned doesn't end God's interest in teaching. In fact, just the opposite. When some have difficulty learning a concept via the first teaching method, another mode must be undertaken. Christ's actual, physical presence was the first mode; Christ living through us is the second.

God speaks to people where they are and addresses them in ways they can comprehend. Nowhere do we see God saying, as the colleague I told you of earlier did, "Well, I prepared my lecture, and I delivered it. Therefore, I taught. What my students didn't learn was no longer my responsibility." God follows up his teaching; his purpose is not his *teaching* but our *learning*.

All people learn best what they experience. In Luke 7:29–30, we are helped to see the truth of this. Those who were experts in the law but had not been baptized by John rejected God's purpose for their lives. They could not hear Jesus' message with open ears, nor see it with open eyes. On the other hand, those who had been baptized with the baptism of John, having experi-

enced its power firsthand, knew exactly what Christ was saying. His words served to increase their insights, to deepen their
knowledge. They were *enabled* to better understand God's kingdom first by experience and, secondarily, by listening to Christ's
words.

Primary emphasis on actual growth experiences, rather than
attendance at lectures, makes possible the enlightenment that is
crucial to education. Enlightenment comes through experiencing, and it is exactly why the literary light-bulb flashes on above
a comic strip character's head at the moment of insight. "Aha!"
such a character seems to exclaim. "Now I begin to understand." Internalizing makes sense out of words, but in order to
make sense of them, personal intimacy with what they mean
must precede their study. As we have already seen, a person's
ability to learn depends not so much on intellectual exercise as
on emotional receptivity.

The composition of the Bible itself provides additional insight
into the teaching/learning process. For example, the Gospels
repeat many of the same stories, but in different enough ways
that the points become clearer in the retelling. Different transla-
tions, too, in their use of variant synonyms and syntax do much
the same thing with the same story. When one instructional
technique fails to impart enough knowledge to clarify the purpose of teaching, a second must be added to it. In this way (to
cite just one instance in which we can see this happening),
Matthew and Mark both give us a detailed account of Jesus'
startling walk on the water—though the choice of details included differs slightly (Matt. 14:22–33; Mark 6:45–52, RSV).

In both accounts, Jesus tells the disciples, "Take heart, it is I;
have no fear." But only in Matthew do we get Peter's response,
"Lord, if it is you, bid me come to you on the water." Thus, only
in Matthew do we see Peter's new grasp on faith and its almost
simultaneous faltering as he steps out, then sinks, into the
waves. In faith, Peter could walk side by side with his Lord; in
doubt, he had no such capability. Jesus, of course, immediately
reaches out his hand to save Peter, and as the wind ceases, those
in the boat say worshipfully, "Truly you are the Son of God."

Mark gives us more of a complete background on why Jesus walked out to the boat in the first place: "When evening came, the boat [with the disciples in it] was out on the sea, and [Jesus] was alone on the land [where he had been praying]. And he saw that they were distressed in rowing, for the wind was against them. . . . He came to them, walking on the sea." Jesus' concern for his disciples was ever ready.

But through each writer's revelations of the same story—and this is what's important to us—we gain a deeper understanding of the man Jesus Christ. Through their repetitive and yet differing natures, each account helps consummate our desire to know, our curiosity for learning what might otherwise elude our grasp. Through having access to more than one perspective, we are able to "round out" our knowledge of particular incidents and all that is significant about them.

Presenting more than one perspective is both scripturally endorsed and intellectually sound. The first teaching often prepares our hearts for the second, as the Old Testament did for the New. It is a building up and a building toward which is at once wondrous and yet completely necessary. Without the building aspect of teaching, learning remains superficial and easily forgotten. Systematic "building" sparks the connections among those billions of neurons waiting within our brains for just such ignition.

Interrelationships: Instruction, Learning, and Forgetting

Do you spell the word for disconnection *separate* or *seperate*? And if you aren't certain which spelling is right, do you have a remembering problem, or a forgetting problem?

Actually, you have a forgetting problem. That is, your brain is so efficient it "hangs onto" the incorrect spelling long after you have learned the correct spelling. Thus, every time you want to use the word, your memory dredges up both spellings for you again, compounding your communication confusion for years to come. It is not a remembering problem, since to your everlasting bemusement you can remember both possible spellings. Even though you realize one is wrong, you have difficulty recalling which one it is. No, it is, instead, a *forgetting* problem, because you are unable to forget the spelling you would like to forget.

In a small way, this illustration exemplifies the relationship between learning and forgetting and how the power of the brain affects both. Sometimes, as with common misspellings, it may seem as if your brain is too efficient for your own good. "Pursuit of knowledge under difficulties, Sammy?" queries Charles Dickens in *The Pickwick Papers*.

On the other hand, if our brains are this efficient, and if they store so much irrelevant (as well, of course, as relevant) information, how come there are so many things we can't remember? Why do many of us forget things we want to remember? And why are games like "Trivial Pursuit" so popular with young and old alike? Knowledge of the characteristics of memory can be of considerable value to teachers as they seek to become enablers of learning.

There are at least five basic theories about why we forget: fading theory, distortion theory, suppression theory, interference theory, and poor retrieval theory. In the fading theory, we are believed to lose from memory material we don't frequently bring to mind. That's why "Trivial Pursuit" fascinates us. We know we know many of the answers to the questions— at least, we used to know them—but pulling them out of our distant pasts is the frequently unsuccessful challenge. Information has to be repeated, or brought to mind again, in order for it to stay in long-term memory.

Distortion theory, as explained by Guy Lefrancois, goes something like this: "It is now difficult for me to remember a specific sunset accurately, because I have seen so many that even the most striking ones have become distorted until in my memory of sunsets there isn't a single one that looks very different from any other. It's sad but true. My sunrises fare better, probably because I haven't seen as many."[6] Memory fades, but what doesn't fade entirely becomes distorted through the passage of time. It becomes lost under other material, takes on similarities to that material, and eventually is indistinguishable from the other.

Suppression theory involves the idea that people tend to forget events that are particularly unpleasant. Unpleasantness trickles into the subconscious mind where it is not exactly forgotten but where the individual is no longer consciously aware of it either. The brain provides a basic survival mechanism, a certain psychological protectiveness against painful memories. However, recollected pain can continue to infiltrate our conscious mind, triggered by sights and smells and sounds which recall it for us when we might least expect it. Only Christ, as we saw earlier, can totally heal us of these hurtful memories.

The most popular current theory of forgetting is set forth in the interference theory. This is the idea that interference from previous or subsequent learning is a prevalent cause of forgetting. Teachers illustrate this theory themselves in their recall, or lack of recall, of students' names. Teachers may have difficulty remembering the names of new students, particularly if they have been teaching for awhile and have known many students with similar names. Confusion of old names with new faces is a result. By the same token, once teachers have learned all the names of their new students, they may have difficulty remembering the names of former students. Interference, or a confusion of old and new learnings, results in forgetting.

The last theory, the poor retrieval theory, has its roots in psychological study where it is maintained that people never "forget" per se. What they do is fail to develop an efficient system of retrieval. They merely appear not to remember because they are unable to find a way of recalling an item of information from memory. It's there, but they don't possess the proper retrieval cues.

Danger Ahead: A Trend Toward "Teacher-Proofing"

Even though we can look at theories that affect classroom interaction, teaching itself is virtually impossible to describe. At least, it is impossible to describe simply. The activity of teaching is highly complex and influenced by an incredible array of variables. Because of teaching's manifold activities, it is difficult to draw a generalized conclusion about who is or is not a "good teacher."

It is a bit easier to determine what learning is. After all, certain types of learning (unlike teaching) can be measured through carefully structured tests. Because students either know, or don't know, various items of information, it is beginning to be believed that teaching can be similarly measured. This is based on the notion that if students learn (or if they can answer questions correctly), then teaching has happened. Likewise, if students haven't learned (or if they don't answer test questions appropriately), teaching has "obviously" not happened. In truth, teaching may not have happened in either instance, or it might very well have happened in both.

What is missing in this teaching-to-learning ratio is the "incredible array of variables" that influence life in classrooms. But it is being clutched at as a way for parents and school administrators to "get a handle on" the nebulous area of whether teachers are effective or not. It has even been given a name: teacher accountability. Nothing is wrong, of course, with teachers being accountable for what they do in classrooms to and with children. In fact, I would emphatically underscore that it is essential for teachers to be held accountable for all their behaviors.

The danger is in assuming that certain academic learnings must be "guaranteeable" via direct teacher action. What this really means is that teacher accountability is no longer the main issue. Increasingly, the main issue is the demand for assurance that particular kinds of learning will occur, no matter what. How do we make certain Johnny or Susie will learn $2 + 2 = 4$ in first grade if it cannot directly be made a part of the teacher's contract? Well, we'll write it into the curriculum guide, that's how. And we'll give the teacher no authority (and, more important, no *way*) to tamper with the curriculum guidelines we've adopted.

We are reaching an era in education when we are looking for

systems that will, in essence, "teacher-proof" our children's classrooms. If the teacher can be an adverse influence on students' learning (and it is acknowledged by most that this possibility exists), then isn't it better for a teacher simply to be superfluous? Just in case the teacher *won't* (for whatever reasons) do an adequate job of teaching $2 + 2 = 4$ in the first grade, we'll make certain the teacher will have no impact of any kind on Johnny and Susie. That way, what happens in schools will become "automatic," and we'll no longer have to worry about school failure. Will we?

In *The Technology of Teaching*, B. F. Skinner advocated automating teaching. He argued that those who say "we learn by experience" and those who say "we learn by doing" and those who say "we learn by trial and error" are like the three blind men holding, respectively, the tusks, trunk, and tail of the elephant. Each assumes that a little bit of truth is the whole truth. Learning involves (1) the occasion upon which the behavior occurs, (2) the behavior itself, and (3) the consequences of the behavior. This is the whole elephant. Learning by experience emphasizes the occasion; learning by doing, the behavior; and learning by trial and error, the consequences. In this context, the teacher provides the first and third elements of teaching, and the student provides the second. Skinner expressed concern over teachers' capability to carry out their two-thirds of this formula effectively for each of their, say, thirty students. He didn't see it as *humanly* possible.[7]

Skinner's is a complex theory that I treat here only on its surface. It is the heart of the teacher-proofing mentality that I want to reach, and in a small way Skinnerian philosophy touches that heart. It is "teaching as a science" exemplified. As long as it is understood that "art" is a verb, to my mind teaching seems eminently more an art than a science. In fact, Harry Dawe, writing for the *Phi Delta Kappan,* calls teaching "a performing art."[8]

My thesis is, and always has been, that people and not proposals are the answer for schools. I do not, then, see teachers as needing to be "written out" of schools in some misguided effort to homogenize learning situations and protect children from incompetence. On the contrary, I fear the dehumanizing of schools will do more damage than will taking our chances with the individual leadership capabilities of authentic human beings. Only human beings can provide what *must* transpire if a classroom is to become a significant laboratory for learning. (The word "laboratory" is used advisedly and is not in contra' diction to the idea of teaching as an art.)

A facilitator assists students in their learning. In this role, teachers involve students in interaction with content and with other people. They instill in their students a spirit of inquiry by being co-inquirers. They serve as models and assist students in identifying significant questions and interesting problems. They excite students with ideas and foster in them a lifelong desire to go on discovering other ideas. Emotional and social climates can open up a learning environment that will stimulate intellectual activity. Technology or machines or programmed instruction— in a word, teacher-proofing—cannot provide this to a class' room. Only people can.

If we look at the teaching of reading as an illuminator, we see that some children learn to read under all systems devised. And some children fail under every system. Yet a teacher-proof sys' tem has supposedly been designed in the basal (or basic) reading program used in over 95 percent of all elementary schools, pub' lic and private, throughout this country. In order to better un' derstand the benefits and dangers of teacher-proofing, let's examine the advantages of basal readers, and let's also see what their cost to us is.

Basal readers, accompanied by their familiar workbooks, are the mainstay of formal reading programs virtually everywhere across the land. Over the years, basal reading series have re' ceived much criticism from both teachers and interested parties outside of schools. "Dick and Jane" have become cartoon-like parodies for what it means to learn to read. Early basal programs were characterized by dull, limited vocabularies and white, middle-class stereotyping.

The criticisms were justified, and publishers responded by

making major improvements. Actually, basal readers and their related materials are now better than they have ever been. Modern series contain excellent artwork and many selections from fine children's literature, including realistic minority and ethnic experiences.

A beginning teacher can gain confidence in teaching reading by using a basal series. The teacher's guide provides a running script of not only each lesson's objectives but of actual words to use in interaction with students. It is a "no-brainer" exercise, as some of my college students are fond of saying. Any "rum-dum off the street" can do it. Just follow along through the "Now-you-say, now-they-say" playbill, and you've got it: a reading teacher. After examining basal materials, my students invariably ask, "What do we need a college education for? We could save a lot of money if the only requirement for being a reading teacher is following this script. Who needs all these education courses in order to do that?"

Who does, indeed? But not having to worry about what to teach, or how to teach it, is a strong advantage from the teacher's point of view. It makes the job easier. All the decisions are made—the curriculum is "set in cement," as it were. It is impossible to "mess up," and if you do, it's not your fault. You were just "going by the book," as your school demanded of you. But let's not forget the *student's* point of view. Rachel realized it with Lenny, and it's true: when a student's needs conflict with a teacher's, the student's take priority.

Illiteracy, even with twelve years of schooling, is documented all too frequently. But what about aliteracy, the relatively new phenomenon of people who can read but won't? Children in a basal reading program are early taught the "rules" of reading, drilled on a series of phonics skills, introduced to letters and words in isolation, shown that word-perfect reading is essential, discouraged from guessing, and constantly reminded of the importance of reading and the seriousness of falling behind. The term "reading" comes to be associated in students' minds with the daily tasks of reading (often aloud in a group) from the basal reader and doing the assigned workbook pages, as well as the aforementioned stresses. Each day, the same thing, over and over. Thus, when children are asked, "Do you like reading?" they are likely to reply with a curious mixture of confusion, boredom, and tension, "No way, man!"

In the end, we produce from basal reading programs—which are teacher-proofed and not subject to individual whim or interest—a set of adults who either can't read because the skills have been so fragmented that they have never pulled them together, or a set of adults who pulled the isolated skills together but experienced such tediousness in doing it that they reject reading as a recreational activity for the rest of their lives. Only infrequently today does a child spring forth from school with a genuine love of books. The school, of course, does not operate independently from the rest of society, as we've already seen. It survives in the television milieu, as the home does, and it competes with television for a child's attention. So what help could a school provide toward ensuring students' lifelong love affairs with books, given the culture we live in?

For one, I believe that teachers who have no choice but to use basal readers as their primary reading curriculum material can use them in professional and creative ways. Teachers can adapt such materials to fit the needs and abilities of individual children. And teachers can supplement their classroom reading activities with *real* books—that is, library books selected from the world of quality children's literature. Teachers can, and must, read a book, or a portion of a book, aloud every day. "There is no time" is unacceptable as an excuse for not doing so. Whatever is important to a child's literate future is premium in terms of classroom time. And teachers must, as well, incorporate children's own spoken language into written language, either through dictation and transcription or through "creative writing." Since all writing is creative, I prefer other terms, but the idea of generating student writing is what's essential.

Children need exposure to the wonder of language in its many forms. Our goal must be integration. No subject area should be left untouched by reading and writing if we want true literacy to ensue. It is understanding communication in its multifarious forms, and not a study of separate skills (like drilling on the sound of "B" and then, after mastery, the sound of "D"), that ultimately activates our urge to become a vital part of the literate world.

What a pity if, through teacher-proofing classrooms, we inadvertently advocate concealing what matters most! Loss of opportunities to give individual attention could be a serious evil for students in schools, and thus, for our society as a whole.

Facilitation of Learning: Enabling in Action

A college sophomore just entering a teacher education program defined a teacher to me as being "a committed facilitator of learning who knows the course content so well that he or she can call it up in a variety of ways to respond to a student's learning needs." What marvelous insight! And an equally astute freshman told me that "a teacher is someone who has something to give to another, be it knowledge or wisdom or experiences, and has the ability to impart that to another individual—and does it." His inclusion of "and does it" is extremely important to his understanding of his future as a teacher, and to the future of the students who will be in his classroom.

"Doing it" is facilitation of learning, or enabling in action. The ability to impart knowledge or wisdom or experiences is not enough. We all have opportunity to exercise that ability, because we all have an impact on the lives of children through our encounters with them, no matter how brief those encounters may be. We model whether we know it or not, and all of us are, willingly or not, teachers. Having looked at this concept in depth in chapter 1, we must recognize as well that what we do with that ability is quite another thing. How we respond to children's pressing concerns determines our effectiveness as facilitators of learning. Will we take up the mantle and teach confidently, with conviction? Or will we choose to be oblivious to our opportunities for teaching?

Carl Rogers, in debating B. F. Skinner's behaviorist stand on learning, is credited with first pointing out the "learning facilitation" approach to teaching. Rogers criticizes traditional approaches to instruction on several counts. These include the assumption that all students are equally ready for learning, that they can learn in the same amount of time, and that the teacher is the best judge of what is meaningful and necessary for students.[9] In evaluating Rogers's philosophy, Lefrancois says:

> Rogers's view of behavior is, in many ways, an obvious and intuitively correct one. That is, it is obvious that each individual perceives the world in a manner not experienced by anyone else. It is also obvious that, in order to understand others completely, it may be useful to adopt their point of view. . . . Such theorizing can sometimes generate fruitful ideas. . . . The important question now should not be: 'Is this a correct view of humanity?' but simply: 'Is this a useful way of looking at humanity?' Indeed it is.[10]

Rogers presents a strong plea for teaching which is focused upon self-discovered learning. He calls this idea *student-centered teaching*. All schools are concerned with the present and future welfare of students; all recognize the worth and the rights of the individual; all pay "lip service" to such human and humane values as openness, honesty, and selflessness. The conflict between Rogers (or his disciples in humanistic education) and more traditional approaches comes when the pressure of large numbers, regimentation, anonymity, and the striving for academic success leave no time or energy for unpressured communication, exploration of values, or development of self.

Humanistic education, then, emphasizes growth in self-development, communication, and values—all compatible with Christ's perspective on people. More traditional emphases in education are mastery of academic content, good citizenship, and sportsmanship. While these are not incompatible with Christ's teaching, neither are they of primary importance. In-deed, the second three are more capable of coming about after the first three are intact.

In searching for possible problems with humanistic educa-tion, Lefrancois makes this rather amazing pronouncement: "Perhaps the most telling criticism of specific humanistic ap-proaches to teaching is that virtually *all of these approaches are extremely dependent upon the personal qualities and skills of individual teachers. More conventional approaches to classroom practice are, in this respect, much more 'teacher proof'*" (italics mine).[11] After considering the merits of humanistic education, Lefrancois's argument *against* it is—astonishingly—my argu-ment *for* it. Good, healthy teaching is dependent upon the per-sonal qualities and skills of individual teachers.

It is self-evident that the best things that happen to students in schools happen through genuine, caring teachers. We can all cite experiences from our own backgrounds to add weight to this credo. How can teaching-proofing classrooms—in effect, de-humanizing classrooms—be better than having an authentic human being available to work with kids? Obviously it can't be. But, in absence of such authentic human beings, schools are searching for ways to "ensure" excellence without reliance on people. Thus, we have a barrage of proposals designed to "over-come" the personalities of those who administrate them. In fact, it is hardly important who runs these programs, because they are meant "to stand alone," to exist in terms of their own merits. And, of course, the notion behind all of these proposals is that, through their implementation, our schools will regain a tone of excellence.

Unless the nature of people changes (and God has given us no indication that the design for human creation is changing), I hardly think this will happen. Children are people, and they will continue to be distinct individuals who need recognition of their differences, as well as their similarities, in order for them to grow into full maturity. Such perception requires the skills of a willing and able adult. Each classroom is in need of just such a person to act as its learning facilitator.

In setting the stage for learning, a teacher could be like Paula. Paula's elementary classroom is colorful and enticing. No matter where a person sits in it, there is attractiveness and humor and language enrichment to ponder. Paula has gone to a great deal of trouble to make it an appealing room. There are bold little animal creatures peeking out from behind bulletin boards (but always different creatures each month); alphabet antics dance imaginatively around the border of the ceiling; green plants at the window bring the outdoors in no matter what the season; low shelves of books and rocks and other collectibles beg to be looked at and handled; a rug and a rocker add a touch of coziness; a loft is nearby for getaway times; and the name of each student, beautifully written on his or her individual desk, speaks of belongingness. Each morning, Paula stands at the door with a smile and personalized greeting in honor of each student's arrival. She is a teacher who sets an emotional tone in which learning is free to occur. Without needing words, she has said to her students, "You are so special and important that you are worth every moment I invest in the environment we share together. I will continue to explore ways to welcome you to my life. Actually, having you here *is* my life."

In *The Four Loves,* C. S. Lewis makes an important point about the role of enabling when he compares its function to a gardener's:

> It is no disparagement to a garden to say that it will not fence and weed itself, nor prune its own fruit trees, nor roll and cut its own lawns. A garden is a good thing but that is not the sort of goodness it has. It will remain a garden, as distinct from a wilderness, only if someone does all these things to it. Its real glory is of quite a different kind. The very fact that it needs constant weeding and pruning bears witness to that glory. It teems with life. It glows with color and smells like heaven and puts forward at every hour of a summer day beauties which man could never have created and could not even, on his own resources, have imagined.[12]

Children's lives are our garden. They will remain a garden, as distinct from a wilderness, only if someone cultivates them. But they bear witness to God's glory in the very fact that they need this cultivation, this "weeding and pruning," for, like a garden, they teem with life. And, like a garden, they will surpass our expectations for them *if* they are enabled to do so.

CHAPTER FIVE

I Can't Do That—
Go Ask Someone Else, O.K.?

THE NEED FOR PRODDERS

The tragedy of life
is not so much what men suffer,
but rather what they miss.

—Thomas Carlyle—

I have a dear friend who is a respected teacher and accomplished
writer. He exemplifies in my life what this chapter is all about.
Throughout the writing of this book, he has been my steadfast
exhorter and onward-prodder. Sometimes his prodding has re-
sulted in my exhausted tears and adamant protestations. Occasionally I have viewed him as unfeeling and harsh. Often I have
wondered if I had it in me to do what he wanted me to do. But
he seems to know the part of me that's hidden inside, to recognize what my limits truly are, and he won't let me get away
without exploring them to their fullest. Always he has helped
me be better than I thought I could be. In truth, he has known
more about what I'm capable of than I have.

His belief in the importance of what I have wanted to communicate has impelled me toward the creation of a book which,

except for him, might have continued to exist only inside my head. It was his forcefulness that drove it out into the open. I'd rail at him that he was "writing" for me, via personal example, the chapter on the need for prodders. He'd laugh when I'd say that—laughing off my concerns is his forte—and then, amused, he would blithely send me off for another rewrite. My friend calls this "living on the edge of adventure."

Uncharted Territory: Living "Adventurously"

One time I drove our family car behind my husband, who drove the U-Haul truck packed with all our belongings, to a new home. What I saw for hundreds of miles was the words stenciled across the back of that truck: AN ADVENTURE IN MOVING. Fatigued and stressed, as moves invariably make me, I raged against the cavalier assumption that this was an adventure. The sign became increasingly irritating to me throughout the trip, and I took out my annoyance on Fred at stops along the way. After all, he was the one who had rented the truck and "forced" me to stare at its falsely enthusiastic tidings for mile after interminable mile. How dare anyone presume to tell me this was an *adventure* in moving, or an adventure in anything else, for that matter! It did not fit into my conception of "adventure."

And yet it did. Maybe the *act* of moving wasn't particularly adventurous—it was, as I knew it to be, both exhausting and stressful—but through the move, we opened our lives to experiencing something remarkable that no road map could lead us toward. The move carried us into a realm which could only become part of our lives if we risked saying "yes" to opportunity. And until we placed ourselves on the edge of the unknown, we could not hope to reach the center. New friends, new challenges, new growths and insights, and a better understanding of our place in God's kingdom waited for us in that center. "No risk, no reward," as my madcap son frequently declares.

This is not to say that we must always physically move from one place to another in order for all this to occur—far from it! But it is true that we must push ourselves into exploring new opportunities, whatever or wherever those opportunities might be. If we stay only in the world comfortably familiar to us, and thereby, secure in its familiarity, we may miss something important in God's plan for our lives. In fact, it is difficult to think of times when God has allowed those he commissions to remain in their snug little niches. He is the Ultimate Prodder, and he is not averse to dragging us, kicking and screaming, toward whatever "adventure" he has in mind for us.

Our son, Marc, prodded us toward a new adventure recently. Marc is a zealous student of the German language. He studies it and loves it and intends to become fluent in it. In about the middle of his sophomore year in high school, he began thinking how interesting it would be to have a German exchange student live with us for a year. Finally, he got up the nerve to broach the subject to his father and me. I must say, as Marc rather expected, we embraced the idea less than enthusiastically. We are a busy, involved family, and we had several concerns about fitting an exchange student into our already-existing lifestyle. We were comfortable with the way things were.

When our sons ask us something we are uncertain about, our standard answer goes a bit along the lines of, "We'll think about it." They both know that reply is our euphemism for, "Don't waste your time hoping." Nevertheless, taking us at our less-than-sincere word, Marc gave me the telephone number of the place to call for further information about "adopting" an international student. And I said, "O.K., thanks," probably inadvertently cuing him to keep after me.

Every few weeks after that, Marc would inquire to see if I'd called yet to get more information. In honesty, I would have to reply, "No." Then Marc would ask pleasantly, "Well, when are you going to?" He convinced me, by never letting loose of the idea and through a barrage of gentlemanly reminders, that this was important to him, that he was serious about this idea.

So, I called for information. Anyway, by the time we had a seventeen-year-old German boy assigned to us for the next school year, I may have even outdistanced Marc in excitement at the prospect. The enriching adventure of crossing cultural bonds was made possible for many through the prodding of one.

Because of others propelling me away from the inertia of complacency throughout the past years, my life has been much more interesting for me. And it is similar prodding that is necessary in schools, too, if students are to begin understanding what life can hold for them.

Teaching Something Tough: Prodding's Imperative

Sometimes when we think of "demanding" teachers, we do so in negative terms. Actually, a teacher who demands the right kinds of things of kids could be the best friend those kids will have. A teacher who prods and pushes and even pulls things from her or his students and who does so in the context of modeling and loving, of healing and enabling, is a marvelous addition to any school faculty.

Paul, changed from Saul through God's display of dramatic prodding, would never regret the forcefulness of his Teacher's drive to make him better. How could he? It was difficult for Paul to believe God could love him and single him out for leadership in spite of all he had done to hurt God. Yet, once Paul accepted the truth of that amazing love, his life was forever changed.

With love intact—and with the nature of that love unquestioned by students—dramatic examples of growth are free to occur. Few things are as enhancing to one's self-esteem as the acquisition of knowledge. Knowing that we know things is valuable to building confidence in ourselves and in our responsibilities. Teaching something tough becomes an essential learning tool in classrooms.

Jan is an English teacher. She works in an alternative high school with a student body composed primarily of teens who, for one reason or another, have not succeeded in regular classrooms. Through years filled with a steady pattern of school failure, most of these teens are deeply troubled, embittered, and angry. Many have become hardened delinquents who no longer respect authority of any kind. Jan's teaching assignment is a recognizably difficult one.

Yet the way Jan handles it might seem incongruous to some. Her academic goals for her students are high. That is, scholastically she does not coddle her students. She views herself as their last chance. In her view, what they don't need is "mothering," or a lessening of expectations, so much as it is attainment of self-worth through knowing they have met tough standards. And it is this type of self-worth that she intends they will take from her classroom.

Jan has lived long enough to know it's a hard, often cruel, world. She knows that her students, through experience and not years, have learned that as well. They have responded to what they have seen by putting around themselves a protective veneer of toughness. They have encased themselves in a shell of ferocity. It is the only way they know how to survive, and it is probably the most evident characteristic about the students at Jan's school. If adults have told them they are incorrigible, Jan will teach them how to spell it. While she's at it, to capitalize on the graphic similarities of the two words, she'll also teach her students about the spelling and meaning of incorruptibility.

In Jan's class, students will write poetry. They will voice their thoughts and innermost feelings in a number of expressive ways. And in the process of revising and editing these writings, Jan will demand flawless spelling, punctuation, and usage as an end product. She will demand dictionary and thesaurus skills and familiarity with other reference devices to stretch vocabulary and thinking. Obscenities are outlawed not just because they are obscenities but because they limit the ability to communicate.

She meets with each student individually every other week. Through talks and contracts with Jan, these "slow, incorrigible" students will be guided into writing term papers, and they will do so with footnoted research. They will deal with topics like "Egypt: Ancient Land in Modern Times" and "An Ecological Mystery: Who *Really* Killed Cock Robin?" They will write on abortion and organized crime and Australian film-making, on pornography and democracy and the wisdom of William Shakespeare.

Because Jan is a "demanding" teacher, because she dares to teach something tough to students thought to be themselves too tough to care about academic niceties, her students are rewarded with knowledge of the world and with the realization that they are able citizens functioning in it. Pride in intellectual capacities is gradually restored. She tries to send her students from her with a new excitement for learning. Certainly Jan has frustrations and even some failures too, but there are also rewards. Many of her students go on to enroll in advanced educational pursuits, and many come back to see her, year after year, their lives testimony to effort and purpose.

Other teachers, too, frequently try to have some time alone with individual students, but the teacher-student dialogue is often undertaken in public rather than private. A roomful of students may be listening attentively to these personal dialogues, or other students may be engaged in their own activities while still within earshot. Either way, privacy escapes. God met Moses in private by the burning bush. God did not choose a moment when others were nearby. He sought out Moses alone, for a one-on-one confrontation.

Private conversations between a teacher and student are more beneficial than public ones for several reasons. First, there are fewer interruptions. A teacher and student can concentrate without distraction on what each is saying to the other. In addition, nonverbal signs of encouragement and affirmation (smiling, laughing, a pat on the head or shoulder) are more naturally given. A teacher who shows genuine personal concern for an individual student is more likely to have a beneficial, even dramatic, influence on that student's behavior, just as God did with Paul and Moses and many, many others. In a real sense, there is no escaping the prodding of a teacher who has singled you out for special attention.

God: "The Hound of Heaven"

Peter and Thomas both knew what it was to be singled out. John 21 tells of a special moment with Christ that is provided for Peter, a special disciple. After the resurrection, Jesus enables the disciples to catch some 153 fish, which just moments before had eluded their nets. Once dead, now alive, Christ is still involved in the particulars of his disciples' everyday world. Immediately after this amazing act, Peter is singled out. With the shame of his denial still fresh in his mind, Peter finds himself lovingly reinstated by the resurrected Christ. After that, Peter follows Jesus with unwavering devotion, his firm faith carrying him through his own head-down crucifixion.

Christ singles out Thomas, too, by providing a "viewing" of his resurrected body that was planned just for the doubting disciple because Thomas had missed the earlier one. "Then he said to Thomas, 'Put your finger here; see my hands. Reach out your hand and put it into my side. Stop doubting and believe'" (John 20:27, NIV). Christ prods Thomas into doing something Thomas was reluctant to do. And because he had been reluctant, his ability to comprehend was limited. But when Thomas responds to Christ's demand of him, he receives new insight. "My Lord and my God!" is his amazed, wonder-filled cry.

Scripture is replete with examples of God's prodding. From the Old Testament's Abraham, who was pushed into becoming the "father of many nations," and Moses, who became at God's behest the deliverer of the enslaved Israelites, to the New Testament's Peter, sent far away to minister to the Gentiles, and Paul, chosen for preaching even with a personal history behind him of murder and public persecution of Christians, God prods people in directions they never expect to go, and think they cannot go.

It is with the accuracy of divine insight that poet Francis Thompson labels God "The Hound of Heaven."

On and on go examples of God's "hounding." Hosea, an Old Testament prophet whose words are recorded in the book of the Bible bearing his name, married a prostitute at God's command. He bought her for fifteen shekels and a bushel-and-a-half of barley, and yet, despite her background and continuing infidelities, Hosea grew to love her very much. Through God's pushing, and through Hosea's openness to respond to that pushing, Hosea is allowed the great privilege of symbolizing Christ's enduring love for us. Hosea is even given the choice plum of prophesying Christ's coming triumph over death. He was the first to voice the question, "Where, O Death, is your sting?" (Hos. 13:14, NIV), a question which was later echoed by Paul in the New Testament (1 Cor. 15:55, NIV). In worldly terms, Hosea was a nobody. But God pushes otherwise nondescript people into accomplishing amazing acts. The whole Book of Acts is devoted to just such accounts.

The glorious truth is that Jesus need not be available to others in the flesh in order for the miracles we associate with his physical presence to occur. His program is not dependent on his carrying it out. He has commissioned others to do the work as his stand-ins. He prodded the disciples, and he prods us toward this very end. "When Jesus had called the Twelve together, he gave them power and authority to drive out all demons and to cure diseases, and he sent them out to preach the kingdom of God and to heal the sick" (Luke 9:1–2, NIV). Later in this same chapter, when John says, "Master, we saw a man driving out demons in your name and we tried to stop him, because he is not one of us," Jesus reproves John. "Do not stop him," Jesus said, "for whoever is not against you is for you" (Luke 9:49–50, NIV).

"After this the Lord appointed seventy-two others and sent them two by two ahead of him to every town and place where he was about to go. He told them, 'The harvest is plentiful, but the workers are few. Ask the Lord of the harvest, therefore, to send out workers into his harvest field. Go! I am sending you out like lambs among wolves'" (Luke 10:1–3, NIV). Now, it is not altogether calming to contemplate being a lamb among wolves. But those "wolves," without Jesus' actually being there, listened to the "lambs" who carried Christ's power with them. "The seventy-two returned with joy and said, 'Lord, even the demons submit to us in your name'" (Luke 10:17, NIV). When we are prodded by God, we are capable of accomplishing things we never dreamed we could accomplish. When we do it in Christ's name, we act with his power.

The Great Commission was issued to all of us by Christ after his death. When it was no longer possible for him to be physically present with those who needed what he had to bring them, Jesus passed on the privilege and responsibility to those of us who claim our place as his followers and heirs. "All authority in heaven and on earth has been given to me," he said from the mountaintop, before his ascension to the Father. "Therefore, go and make disciples of all nations, baptizing them in the name of the Father and of the Son and of the Holy Spirit, and teaching them to obey everything I have commanded you. And surely I will be with you always, to the very end of the age" (Matt. 28:18–20, NIV).

The way of Jesus often appears upside down or backwards in contrast to the prevailing value system that our minds have absorbed so thoroughly. The Great Commission can be a somewhat intimidating prod for those of us who seek to follow Christ. How do we carry out Christ's instructions of old in today's world?

In an aptly titled book, Donald Kraybill calls God's expectations *The Upside-Down Kingdom*. If it does anything, the kingdom of God shatters most of the assumptions which govern our life. Time and again, in parables, sermons, and acts, Jesus startles us. Things are not like they are supposed to be. The stories don't end as we expect. "Paradox, irony, and surprise permeate the life of Jesus," Kraybill observes. "The least are the greatest. The immoral receive forgiveness and blessing. Adults become like children. The religious miss the heavenly banquet. The pious receive curses. Things are just not like we think they should be."[1]

That this should be so is one of the surest signs that Jesus is continually pushing us toward new conceptions of ourselves and what we should be doing with our lives. He does not allow us to rest in our beliefs for long. When one directive is under-taken, another looms larger. Christ is a serious taskmaster who will not leave us alone. He is constantly pushing us to our outer limits, to the threshold of adventurous living that we're not certain we want to cross. The path beyond seems too dark and choked with mysterious undergrowth.

I do not believe Jesus does this just so our own characters will develop more righteously. If a distinction were to be made be-tween personal and social ethics, it would suggest that decisions which are personal do not have social implications or conse-quences. But, as individuals, we do not operate in a social vacuum. Jesus is not concerned just with our inner natures, or all of those attributes of self which are sealed off from public exposure like attitudes, motives, feelings, emotions, personality traits, integrity, and the like. He does not touch just our separate emotional outlooks and philosophies. He is after our actions. We are expected to "perform" in a certain way. Enabling learn-ing is not enough for God. We are prodded into doing some-thing concrete with what we have been taught. Our actions will not save us, but they may save others.

This does not mean that we should adopt the "sentimentalist mentality of simply 'walking in his footsteps,'" as Kraybill puts it, but it does suggest that Jesus' way of behaving has some impact on how we link the first and the twentieth centuries. And it does suggest something important for how teachers must function with their students in the needy schools of the modern world.

Potential and Possibility: Dealing with Exceptionality

Behaviorism, or teaching as a science, is sometimes called "outside-in" teaching. It is based on the idea that a system of external rewards and punishments will bring about learning. Humanism, or teaching as an art, is conversely labeled "inside-out" teaching. In it, learning is believed to occur by calling on an individual's own internal needs and motivations.

If we believe that a person has intrinsic worth, then we know that every normal child has the potential to be fully a person, just as every normal acorn has the potential to be fully an oak tree and every normal puppy has the potential to be fully a dog. The basic work of a child is to become an adult, and the basic work of a teacher or parent is to help the child do so. Interestingly, in *How to Survive in Your Native Land* James Herndon writes that "the only thing [a famous rat psychologist] could discover in ten years which made rats any smarter was 'to allow them to roam at random in a spacious and variegated environment.' "[2]

Prominent educator Maria Montessori contrasts the difference between external and internal approaches to teaching by advocating a new reliance on the "calling forth" of intrinsic motivation:

> We may liken the child to a clock, and may say that with the old time way it is very much as if we were to hold the wheels of the clock quiet and move the hands about the clock face with our fingers. The hands will continue to circle the dial just so long as we apply, through our fingers, the necessary motor force. . . . The new method, instead, may be compared to the process of winding, which sets the entire mechanism in motion.[3]

If adult care-givers are to facilitate growth in children, we must have a basic faith in growth's possibilities. Educational psychologist Lambert Gardiner points out that we "tend to have this faith for the first nine months of growth (we accept the miracle of birth with surprising casualness) but then [we] lose the faith."[4] Some of the factors inside children waiting for someone with faith to trigger their growth are inherent talent, creativity, and aptitude.

Intellectually gifted children, for instance, are often behavior problems in school. In fact, they are usually not even those students who get the most A's. Children in the superior I.Q. range (130 and above) are more frequently bored in school than they are not, and because boredom does not spur growth, they exercise their considerable mental energies in other, often less acceptable ways. This causes a great deal of misunderstanding and even disbelief among school professionals regarding the true qualities of giftedness. Most adults, whether educators or not, are bewildered by the inherent mental constitution of an ex-tremely bright youngster.

Jude was a problem first-grader who was the despair of his teacher. He played incessantly with his pencil, drumming it on his desk, throwing it in the air, writing on his skin, and once even permanently tattooing the area above his eyebrow with a strong but unintentional thrust. He dawdled over his work, usually never completing it. He sang to himself and clowned for his friends. His joy in going to school was in devising ways to get others to laugh at his antics.

The teacher, frustrated with Jude's lack of work perfor-mance, as well as with his abundance of non-work "perfor-mances," sent him down to the principal's office to get him away from the other children. Actually, she didn't mind getting him away from her either.

The principal, Mr. Gentz, had been around for a lot of years. He recognized an intelligent, bored kid when he saw one. Jude didn't want to be counting how many bluebirds there were on the page; he wanted to know how much change he would get back if he paid for an ice cream with a five-dollar bill. He didn't want to practice writing a paper filled with J's just because that was the letter of the beginning of his name; he wanted to learn how to write a sign that would tell his sister to keep out of his room. Mr. Gentz talked with Jude gently and sympathetically and was unsurprised to discover all this.

Mr. Gentz began inviting Jude down to his office on a regular basis. Both Jude and Jude's teacher looked forward to these scheduled visits. In fact, Jude spent part of every week of his first grade year in the principal's office. To Jude, it was an honor to be there. His complete conviction that this was so convinced his classmates that Jude must be right, and they began to wish they could go to the principal's office too. But the teacher, to the relief of all but Jude's parents, very seldom sent anyone else in the class to Mr. Gentz.

Jude's parents, after some initial concern, began to see an improvement in Jude's schoolwork. Mr. Gentz told Jude he couldn't come to the office until his work in his classroom was completed satisfactorily. As long as Mr. Gentz got good reports from Jude's teacher about his assignments, Jude was free to come to the principal's office. Jude made certain his work didn't interfere with his visits to Mr. Gentz. He polished off his assignments with natural aplomb.

Sometimes Jude sat on Mr. Gentz's lap in the big principal's chair, and sometimes if Mr. Gentz was busy elsewhere in the building, Jude got to sit in it by himself and construct things at the broad walnut desk. Sometimes Jude helped Mr. Gentz by reading lists of names or numbers aloud while Mr. Gentz jotted down corresponding notes. Frequently, Jude was asked what he would like to do during their upcoming time together. They would work out what was feasible and what was not, given Mr. Gentz's other responsibilities.

Always Mr. Gentz had a book waiting for Jude to read. When Jude was finished, Mr. Gentz would obtain another one from the school librarian for Jude's next visit. As the year progressed, Mr. Gentz's selection went to ever more difficult titles. Sometimes they read the stories together; more often, Jude read them silently while Mr. Gentz worked.

It does not overstate the importance Mr. Gentz played in Jude's life to say Mr. Gentz was an emotional and intellectual life-saver for Jude. He broke a negative behavior pattern that was developing in a very capable student, but he did so in creative and perhaps unorthodox and certainly non-traditional ways. Through understatement and acceptance, Mr. Gentz gently prodded Jude toward a recognition of his own potential to accomplish various tasks. Mr. Gentz practiced "inside-out" teaching. Jude's classroom teacher, on the other hand, was unsuccessfully attempting to impose external force on a child who was internally unprepared to deal with it. This was the "outside-in" variety of teaching. Jude, today an adult, knows which one had staying power.

Courage to Risk: Unifying Differences

A teacher I had never met before and who had my son only for a brief period each day in her classroom once said to me, "I *love* your son!"

This was a double-strength invitation if I ever heard one. It would have meant a lot to Kyle to have had a teacher say this to him directly. It meant even more to him to hear from me that she had said it *about* him. Thus, her words were doubly strong in their impact on him.

We have already seen that intentional invitations issued by teachers to students leave more of an impression on student learning than anything else that transpires in classroom life. These invitations are even stronger when they are offered to an individual personally, by "name." Each of us is a unique individual. Each of us has components in us that are to be found only in us. There is no other in the world like me; there is no other in the world like you. Excellent teachers constantly seek out the uniquenesses of their students in an effort to use those uniquenesses purposefully.

God reminds us of his love for variety through his creation of snowflakes. Through snowflakes and leaves and even the structure of every bird's feather, God demonstrates one enduring thing: He loves differences. If we follow his example, we should love them too. He could not have intended for those differences to be eradicated, or why create such an abundance of them? He does intend, I believe, to allow our differences to help us better understand our similarities, or those things which ultimately unify us as human beings.

When it is snowing, unless we look closely we can't see the differences in each individual flake that drifts down to pile up with the others. The reason a close look is worth the effort it takes is not so that you can alter each flake you see, making it the same as every other one blanketing the yard. Obviously the task would be frustrating in its very futility.

The real reason it's important to look closely at each separate snowflake is that in the process you are better able to marvel, wonder at, and appreciate the intricacy and infinite delicacy of the amazing differences among snowflakes. Absolutely no two are ever alike. Still, as those who live in seasonal climates know, it is possible to pack all the flakes into a single ball and send them flying together on a well-directed trajectory. The differences can be unified, at the same time that they remain different. It just has to be prodded into happening, that's all. Someone has to take the time to pack the flakes together.

I know a teacher who "packed the flakes together" (no pun intended!) through stressing individuality in her classroom. Annie instituted a program in her fifth grade room she calls "Star of the Week." Each child in the classroom is scheduled to "star" during one week in the year. The "star" is given a bulletin board in his or her honor, depicting the things about his or her life that the student would like to share: photographs of infancy and childhood, a map showing a record of family moves (or a geographic life history), personal "artifacts" of importance like a soccer jersey or the cover from a favorite book or something representing a treasured family tradition.

The parents, grandparents, and other relatives of the "star" are invited to the classroom on the actual day of presentation (the display itself stays in the room for a week). These family members are encouraged to take part as both spectators and participants. A question and answer time is scheduled after the student being focused upon explains all that he or she has brought. In this sense, it is a sophisticated form of show-and-tell. But the real *pièce de résistance* is that every child in the room, one at a time, is required to tell something each one likes or finds

interesting about their "starring" classmate. It is strength bom-
bardment of the niftiest, most psychologically enriching kind.
These children grow to appreciate what makes others interesting as individuals through their very differentness. Yet the process of focusing on individuality actually unifies the class into
an indivisible community. The students grow to care for each
other in strong ways, and the bonding between them solidifies
immutably.

Annie knows one of the secrets to prodding her students into
uncharted territory. It is taking friends along with you on the
journey.

Questioning: Approach to Self-Discovery

This brings up another of the most important ways to prod
growth in classrooms: questioning techniques. Of all teaching
methods, none is more potentially powerful than questioning.
Many teachers, however, believe that the function of questioning is to test students' knowledge at the end of a lesson. Postman
and Weingartner say it well in *Teaching as a Subversive
Activity*:

> Examine the types of questions teachers ask in classrooms, and
> you will find that most of them are what might technically be called
> 'convergent questions,' but which might more simply be called
> 'guess what I'm thinking' questions. . . . So what students mostly
> do in class is guess what the teacher wants them to say. Conse-
> quently, they must try to supply the right answer.[5]

But what if we taught that sometimes there are no right
answers? What if, like Kipling's Elephant's Child, we asked "a
new fine question that had never been asked before?" What if
we asked what the crocodile has for dinner and *didn't already
know the answer ourselves?* Under this premise, teaching could
indeed become a "subversive activity." We could overthrow
preconceived notions and even push the "kingdom upside-

down" in our quest to live adventurously—which is to say, to live where self-discovery and true knowledge await.

Questioning in classrooms has been studied extensively by many educators and other interested scholars. Taxonomies have been built around the types of questions that must be asked for deepening understandings to occur in learners. These tax-onomies are useful because they heighten our awareness of the need to move beyond literal-level to higher-order types of ques-tions. Since comprehension is more frequently tested at the literal-level (i.e., "How many bears lived in the cottage that Goldilocks visited?"), brain cells are not exactly over-worked in their effort to supply an answer. Obviously it is easier to con-struct questions that are clearly right or clearly wrong, but by doing so we focus on the bottom end of these questioning tax-onomies. Lower-level questions are those which embody strict recall of facts in their answers.

We must not fall into the trap of asking only fact-based ques-tions, or students' ability to think will be greatly impaired. Much better, for future productive reasoning, to ask, "Was it all right for Goldilocks to enter the bears' cottage? Why?" or "What would you have done when the chair broke? What would you have done if you woke up and three bears were staring down at you?" Yet answers to these are not easily tested for accuracy of response. Indeed, who is to say that one response is wrong and another right?

I once heard a speaker illustrate the inappropriateness of cer-tain questions in a way which has stuck with me. He drew our attention to the film *Kramer vs. Kramer,* which was then play-ing in theaters all across the country. "Do you remember the scene in the kitchen?" this speaker asked us. "It's the morning after the mother has left, and the father is trying to make break-fast for his son. Remember?"

Yes, those of us familiar with the film conceded that we remembered the scene well.

The speaker helped us refocus it in our minds. "There's this father, remember?" he went on, gently coaxing our brains along.

"And he's trying to cope with a situation he never expected, and he's got this little hungry boy on his hands, and he's not certain what to do with him. But this father, see, he's going to prove he can handle it, right? And so they make French toast, remember? And it's all gooey and there's egg running every-where, and this dad, he's trying to dip the bread in this coffee mug filled with all this egg goop. He's going to cope, by golly!" The speaker chuckled, shaking his head ruefully. "And the son is sitting there, knowing this is never the way Mommy did it, and his eyes are huge as they watch his father's frantic determin-ation and they fill up the screen, those eyes. You got the pic-ture?"

We all had the picture. We could see it plainly. Indeed, we could even feel it. It was one of filmmaking's truly memorable moments.

"O.K., now," this speaker said, his hands spread wide to make the point, "I'm going to test your comprehension. Are you ready?"

We were ready. We knew we *knew* that scene. We couldn't possibly fail the test. The scene had seeped into our emotional consciousness.

"Here's your test," the speaker warned sternly, and then he challenged our understanding of what we had all deemed impor-tant to recall. "What color," he asked his hushed audience, "is the shirt Dustin Hoffman wears in that scene?"

We sat in our chairs, stupefied. Not one person who had seen the film could pass that most basic, literal-level comprehension test. Yet every one of us had "seen" the actor's shirt. This speaker brought home to all of us the vast difference between true comprehension and the ability to recall isolated, mostly inconsequential facts.

Being prodded into mentally exploring unanswerable ques-tions is eminently better for students, if not for those teachers who prefer easy answers. In their recent study of effective ques-tioning techniques, researchers Carin and Sund suggest that what separates the truly brilliant teacher from the average is the talent for posing the right question at the right time.[6] Well-selected questions stimulate active learning. They help students realize that their role in learning is not a passive one, but one of participation.

Browbeating: Prodding Gone Amok

A girl named Dorie was a very capable young lady. When she reached early adolescence, she began exhibiting less of that capability. In fact, while it is not unusual for a twelve-year-old to go through a temporary reversal of previous behavior patterns, Dorie's grades plummeted drastically in the sixth grade.

At the first grading period in late October, Dorie's parents were aghast. This was their straight-A little girl! What had happened to her? They knew she was better than what her report card would indicate. Her determined parents set out to "encourage" Dorie to do what she was capable of doing. They told Dorie she was grounded until the next grading period (which would be in mid-January). In addition, they told her if her grades were not back to their A-level by then, she would be grounded for the rest of the school year as well. She would neither be allowed to fraternize with her friends in person or on the telephone during her grounding confinement.

I can tell you that Dorie's is a "success" story. That is to say, Dorie did get her grades back to straight As by mid-January. I can also tell you that every time I saw Dorie during the second grading period—and indeed, even though her grounding was lifted, every time I saw her throughout the rest of the school year—her eyes darted frantically from side to side, she spoke with a high, rapid, monosyllabic sound, and her hands never ceased their restless twitching and fluttering. She had a peculiar way of shaking one wrist in the air while her elbow remained glued to her side.

A pressured child, even one with the ability to undertake what someone is prodding him or her toward, is not a healthy child, and maybe will not become a stable adult. There are severe dangers if prodding is better defined as browbeating or bludgeoning, if an attempt to operate in another's best interests is more aptly described as harassment and hatefulness.

Psychologist David Elkind reminds us that when "a person's job places him or her in a situation of chronic, unrelieved stress, the end result is what has come to be called 'job burnout.' Usually what happens is that the person loses all enthusiasm for the job, hates to go to work, and is either lethargic and constantly tired or always tense with nervous energy."[7] Physical symptoms accompany these emotional reactions to stress. We often speak of teacher burnout (and we will address this topic at some length in chapter 7), but by no means does this imply *children* are somehow immune from "job burnout." They are no different from us. And we must recognize it is school that provides their primary stress.

In *The Work Stress Connection,* Veninga and Spradley identified five stages inherent in job burnout.[8] We need to examine "job burnout" from a school perspective. The first stage is the "honeymoon" stage. A child begins school eagerly, with anticipation for what is to come. He or she is happy and filled with high expectations for the experience of school. But the endless demands of learning in a nonsupportive environment and the competitive atmosphere of most classrooms force the student to call upon energy reserves which are not always replenished. This moves the youngster into the second stage, or "fuel shortage" stage. The child is running out of steam. In the third stage, there is the appearance of "chronic symptoms" like proneness to accidents and illness, or severe headaches, ulcers and colitis. Chronic symptoms may also appear in the form of behavioral disorders like aggressive bullying or quiet withdrawal. Excessive drug and alcohol use are further symptoms of this stage of burnout, as is chronic cheating.

Left untreated, all of this leads into the fourth stage, which is the "crisis" stage. "In the first stages of school burnout, the initial challenge and excitement are replaced by dissatisfaction and unhappiness which are dealt with in a variety of symptoms, or stress valves. If these stress valves don't work, or if they become overused, a *crisis* can result." In a crisis, stresses are unbearable and symptoms become increasingly severe. The fifth stage, "hitting the wall," is fortunately not all that common because most children, through exhibiting behaviors generally linked to crises, are taken out of the stressful situation before hitting the wall occurs. But when it happens, it can be likened to the experience of a long-distance runner who has used up all the blood sugar stored in the muscles and, dehydrated, literally cannot run another step. The runner becomes dizzy and faint, has muscle paralysis, and sometimes completely collapses.

In schools, this press for success is appearing earlier and earlier. One kindergarten teacher confided to Marie Winn recently that she was "expected by the dictates of the school system to push a lot of curriculum. Kids in our kindergarten can't sit around playing with blocks anymore. We've just managed to squeeze in one hour of free play a week, on Fridays." Winn warns what effect this has:

> The diminished emphasis on fantasy and play and imaginative activities in early childhood education and the increased focus on early academic-skill acquisition have helped to change childhood from a play-centered time of life to one more closely resembling the style of adulthood: purposeful, success-centered, competitive. . . . This decline in play is surely one of the reasons why so many teachers today comment that their third- or fourth-graders act like tired businessmen instead of like children.[9]

Yet authorities of all kinds—psychologists, educators, sociologists, anthropologists—have written for years of the importance and universality of play in every culture around the world. There is a warning here against turning the world upside-down in a way God never intended. Our task is to be cognizant of the warning so we can heed it. In other words, there is a fine line between a genuine need for prodding and granting license for browbeating.

Lilian Katz is an authority on what is basic for young children. In a summation of her address to the Australian Pre-school Association,[10] we can perhaps better see the line that divides the two spectrums of "pushing."

Katz warns that children first have to acquire a deep sense of safety. This doesn't come so much from being loved as *feeling* loved, *feeling* wanted, *feeling* significant. And the emphasis is on how the child, and not the adult, feels.

Second, every child has to have adequate, though not excessive, self-esteem. Such esteem results from evaluation of self against criteria set by the culture in which the child lives. What our society says is important (glossy magazine-type looks, sex appeal, good grades, athletic prowess, and the like) contributes heavily to most children's lack of confidence in themselves. How many can measure up to such a standard?

Third, every child has to feel that his or her life is worth living, is reasonably satisfying, interesting, and authentic. This proposition suggests we must involve children in activities that are real to them, that are significant and intriguing. It does *not* suggest we settle just for what amuses or entertains children. In this, there is an important ingredient for correct prodding.

Fourth, children need adults and older children who help them make sense of their experiences. We'll look at this in greater depth in the next chapter.

Children's fifth basic need is to have access to adults who accept the authority that is theirs by virtue of their greater experience, knowledge, and wisdom. This, too, fits into the area of proper prodding. Authoritative adults are absolutely necessary, but such adults exercise "their very considerable power over the lives of young children with warmth, support, encouragement, and adequate explanations."

Sixth, children need lots of association with adults and older children who exemplify the personal qualities we want them to acquire. Here we have role modeling again, discussed as a necessary component of education in chapter 1.

And, seventh, Katz proposes that children need relationships and experiences with adults who are willing to take a stand on what is worth doing, worth having, worth knowing, and worth caring about. This proposition, which I call "the need for inter-preters," will be given a detailed examination in the next chapter.

Through understanding children's basic needs, we can and must provide correct prodding—and not prodding gone amok.

Futuristics: Vital New Roles for Schools

I'd like to do a little prodding of my own here. All of us interested in the relevance and excellence of schools are, through our interest, involved in the future of education in an important way, whether we have thought specifically in those terms or not. Educating students for their *future* is what educa-tion is all about—or should be.

In *The Mustard Seed Conspiracy,* Tom Sine states emphat-ically that we as Christians can make a difference in tomorrow's troubled world. "Remember the first time God turned the world upside down? He did it with a small band of disciples and almost no resources except the power of God. We dare not underestimate what God can do with our small loaves and fishes if we give ourselves without reservation to his world-changing conspiracy."[11]

Our tendency to avoid action because "I am only one person" is a human failing we must strive to overcome. This type of thinking is harmful, and possibly, even sinful. God has never told us the cost of bringing about needed change comes cheaply. In fact, not only has he demanded total giving from us; he has promised that anything less will produce no results. Still, we are not ready to accept that doing without the comfort and security of our present lifestyle is the only way to win God's fight. Tom Sine calls this a need to awaken "to the new reality that the party is over."

So it is with public schools and our attitude toward them. The party *is* over. We can go back to the traditionalism of years past in education, but we cannot make those things that worked in days gone by still work today. The world has changed too much for carbon-copying to be effective. A wave of nostalgia for "the good old days" is not going to bring about the changes for this and the next generation, no matter how genuine our desire. Indeed, the scope of the society we live in has changed vastly from what it used to be. Schools, sadly, have not even come close to keeping pace with those changes.

In fact, not only have schools not been keeping pace, change occurs so fast that, because of bureaucratic lag-time, most well-meaning attempts to do something about "getting with it and keeping pace" will wind up out-moded before they are ever implemented. The old maxim of "Look before you leap" may have served people reasonably well in the past, but perhaps it is better to now "Leap, and then look if you possibly can." There is enthusiasm for the idea of new ideas, but not for the new ideas themselves. Yet risk is as important for educational institutions as it is for those who are being educated in them.

Change has a cyclical nature, of course. Trends come and go and then come again. The pendulum constantly swings. But each time something reappears it does so in a slightly different guise. We must not pretend that when something returns, it comes in exactly the same form as when we last saw it.

For example, in the late sixties and throughout the freewheeling seventies fewer ongoing sexual relationships than perhaps during any other similar period in history were consummated by marriage. Yet today there is a renewal of commitment to marriage that is hopeful and good. While it is true that people are getting divorced in large numbers, they are also getting married in large numbers. Recognizing an enduring human need to have a meaningful relationship with someone else, people once again are choosing marriage as the context where that has the best chance of happening.

But here's the point I want to make: it is not the same kind of marriage that we saw in the fifties, when numbers were also up. Today's is a very different kind of marriage. Most wives work, for one thing. There are fewer children, for another. Life is more urbanized, family mobility greater, affluence on the rise, career and educational goals increasing in prevalence. On and on we could chronicle the differences between the recovenanted marriages of today and those of the past.

The same is true of schooling. While there is a resurgence of interest in getting rid of the fluff and going back to the basics in education, how the basics are defined must be handled differently than in the past. The world has changed from what it used to be. Survival skills have changed as well. It is higher-order thinking skills that need to be recognized as the new basics in this complex, ever-changing, technologically adaptive world students are sent out to face.

Educators must become strategic planners to keep pace with it all. They must ask questions of relevance ("Are we going in the right direction?") and of effectiveness ("Are we doing the right things?") and of efficiency ("Are we doing things right?"). Improvement is not enough; we have to accomplish *restructuring*.

Part of the solution is dependent on a need to understand what "being fair" means. Being fair does *not* mean, as commonly thought, treating everyone alike. It means giving everyone equal opportunities to develop themselves in their own individual ways. We have trouble, in education and in family life, understanding the difference between these two methods of demonstrating how to "be fair." Every child, for example, does not require the exact same Christmas present as his brother received at a similar age. What if one is interested in conducting scientific experiments and the other is not? Is it unfair to give one a chemistry set but not the other?

We have a developmental sequence to go through in schools if we are to have education evolve into a conducive environment for authentic learning. At present, we are at the bottom of this evolutionary cycle. We are still working with industrial, or "smokestack," schools. The next stage we must go through is what is termed "transitional improvement." Currently there is impetus for reaching this stage with a renewed focus on how best to achieve excellence in education.

But dialogue, in and of itself, will not get us closer to improvement. Only implemented ideas, or risk-taking, will. Only action accomplishes ends. After moving through the transitional improvement stage, we can begin working to attain true restructuring of our schools. The goal of restructuring is to achieve schools, as a last stage, which can be learning communities in the fullest sense. Learning communities are at the top of the developmental ladder. To know what we are aiming for, we must know a learning community's characteristics.

A learning community is decentralized. In order to get big, we must find some way of staying small. Studies have indicated, for instance, that the student/faculty ratio of a learning environment makes more of an impact on college entrance examination scores (like ACTs) than does the quality of teaching.

A learning community is, second, characterized by worker participation. The reason so many teachers leave the profession is not because there are not financial rewards so much as there are not *psychic* rewards. Teachers grow frustrated with their status in the system. There are no career lattices for them, no opportunities for participative management, very little respect (particularly if you are a male teaching in an elementary school where male role models are desperately needed but hard to find), no staff development or in-service training of a meaningful nature, and no opportunities to be curriculum planners. Teachers have very little to say about what is actually taught because, as we've already seen, so many schools have been effectively "teacher-proofed." Psychic rewards do, indeed, have a great deal more to do with professional satisfaction than does salary. Status, as John Gardner points out in *Excellence,* is at the heart of how to achieve worth.

> An excellent plumber is infinitely more admirable than an incompetent philosopher. The society which scorns excellence in plumb-

ing because plumbing is a humble activity and tolerates shoddiness in philosophy because it is an exalted activity will have neither good plumbing nor good philosophy. Neither its pipes nor its theories will hold water.[12]

Third, a learning community provides individualized service. It has moved from limited options to multiple options. It allows people to reach their own internal goals. Here again we see a need for understanding what it means to "be fair." Education is now a lifetime activity, not one that can be "wrapped up" in a given number of years. Most people today can expect to go through six to ten career changes before retirement. That is the rate at which the nature of work is changing. Self-learning will become the leading form of education in the future. Thus, there must be a change in emphasis from teaching facts and theories in schools to that of application and even knowledge creation. It is a scenario of huge and sweeping change. We must get students to think for themselves if they are to survive.

Truly we are in the information-explosion era. There is too much information being delivered too fast for any one person to keep up with it all. Tools for finding what is needed when it is needed become increasingly more important to our understanding of what it takes to be adequately educated.

Fourth, and perhaps most essential, the nature of the teacher/student relationship must change in a true learning community. These are the only two groups truly critical to the welfare of schools. Teachers in these learning communities will be mentors to and co-inquirers with their students. They will be action researchers who determine whether or not certain content and ways of teaching are appropriate. Classrooms will become laboratories for experimenting with different kinds of learning. Teachers will be recognized experts whose knowledge of students' needs is vast. In other words, teachers will be true professionals to whom the welfare of children is fully entrusted, and the current debate over their status in the system will be stilled.

"True professionalism" is an interesting premise. Many people in schools already know what true professionalism encompasses. Others are in need of discovering it.

Educators who have already taken the path toward attaining true professionalism realize they have a stake in determining the quality of educational practice in all schools, and not just their own. These are the educators who share a common desire for involvement and who accept responsibility for making defensible educational decisions. Just as is education itself, so is the development of teachers a continuous process, one that is never finished. But the requirement for continued study and active participation with students is what makes education dynamic and challenging and why, through these learning communities, it will attract committed, thoroughly competent individuals to its ranks.

Our current level—the industrialized "smokestack" schools—are not all bad, of course. Currently in public schools we are doing well with kids who are white, above average in intelligence, and (largely thanks to 1974's Public Law 94–142) with those who fit into the various special education categories covering both physical and mental "handicaps." Those whose needs we are failing to meet in public schools are minorities, intellectually gifted youngsters, those caught between extremely low and average intelligence, and children who speak English as their second language. We are also failing as a whole in the teaching of reading. All curriculum is language-dependent after third grade. If we lose kids in reading, we effectively lose them for everything.

My personal desire is to prod both educators and others (like parents) who are vitally interested in education toward the goal of helping achieve these learning communities. I want us not to be satisfied with cosmetic improvements. I want us to go after complete restructuring. And I want us to know we are not alone: the Ultimate Prodder, the Hound of Heaven, is there beside us to support us and exhort us to turn the world upside-down.

In the same way that students learn best when they are pushed toward adventure, let us not allow others to convince us that the way schooling should occur has "already been discovered." G. K. Chesterton places the necessity of being adventuresome into proper perspective:

> He wished to discover America. His gay and thoughtless friends, who could not understand him, pointed out that America had already been discovered, I think they said by Christopher Columbus, some time ago, and that there were big cities of Anglo-Saxon peoples there already, New York and Boston and so on. But the admiral explained to them, kindly enough, that this had nothing to do with it. They might have discovered America, but he had not.[13]

CHAPTER SIX

Can You Help Me Understand What's Really Important to Know?

THE NEED FOR INTERPRETERS

I will talk of things heavenly or things earthly;
things moral, or things evangelical;
things sacred, or things profane;
things past, or things to come;
things foreign, or things at home;
things more essential, or things circumstantial.

—John Bunyan—

Ellen, a sixth grade student, knew she was supposed to respect her teacher. She knew her teacher demanded that respect. In fact, he seemed to delight in making Ellen and her classmates afraid of him, to make them tremble at his nearness, to lurch at the sound of his voice. That was the way he measured the amount of respect he was generating. He used a harsh and commanding tone, letting the class know he meant business when he spoke. He carried around a yardstick and slapped it down on desks, on chalkboards, and sometimes even on exposed human flesh if he felt the need for more of his class's attention. His students, without a doubt, were going to learn to "respect" authority.

The class was, according to school officials who occasionally passed by it in the hallway, extraordinarily well-behaved. That is, the students were quiet and compliant. The principal, for one, thought the sixth grade teacher was a fine disciplinarian and, on that basis, a fine teacher. The students were models of orderly decorum.

It was the teacher who was volatile, his temper ever-changing, but only someone regularly attending his class would know it. The principal was not a regular attender. What bothered the teacher not at all one day might very well be the unwitting trigger for an angry outburst the next. The class lived with fear and insecurity, and eventually it erupted into a daily dread of going to school.

Ellen would later assert that she believed her teacher felt his role was to be "a governor, patroller, and assigner of textbook pages to keep us busy and him in control. Without exaggeration, I think I can say none of us learned anything the whole year."

I believe Ellen was wrong. I believe everyone in Ellen's class learned plenty that sixth grade year, though their learnings would never be mentioned in a curriculum guide. They learned, in the case of their teacher, that authority figures are perhaps to be "respected" but not to be trusted. In the case of their principal, they learned that authority figures lack true perception, and so, can be manipulated. They learned that a "good" girl or boy is a quiet, docile girl or boy, a person who makes no waves and who goes along with the "rules" whatever those rules, fair or not, might be. Via example, Ellen and her classmates learned that a very low-level moral code organized and controlled the boundaries of their daily existence.

A child can overcome a sixth grade teacher like this one. If we are to examine what makes a healthy personality, we must recognize that it is not all or nothing: trust or mistrust, confidence in self or shame and doubt, and so on. For whatever reasons, every individual acquires some of each of these qualities. What determines the health of personality is the preponderance of favorable qualities over unfavorable.

Perhaps most important to the creation of a healthy personality is the ability to distinguish between what is truly important in life and what is superficial. Sensitive, mature interpreters can help students make these distinctions. It is a matter of ultimate considerations (e.g., What constitutes a good life?) and a question of values (e.g., What is important to know?).

Through enforcement of arbitrary rules, Ellen's teacher interpreted the answers to these questions inappropriately. What is needed are teachers who will do much better. What is needed are teachers who are concerned, first and foremost, with questions of moral justice. In addressing the 1978 graduating class at Harvard University, Alexander Solzhenitsyn said, as if to us: "I have spent all my life under a Communist regime, and I will tell you that a society without any objective legal scale is a terrible one indeed. But a society with no other scale but the legal one is not quite worthy of man either."[1]

Moral Education: A Matter of Values

It is a serious error to speak of public school teaching and assume there is no room in it for moral education simply because a school may not be tied directly to a particular religious organization. There not only is room for moral instruction in education, it is an essential component of all teaching, no matter where that teaching occurs.

It is widely accepted, for example, that public schools have had much influence on the change in the majority culture's perception of blacks that has taken place during the last few decades. Martin Luther King, Jr., gave a stirring and memorable speech during the 1968 Washington Civil Rights March. "I have a dream," he said, "that my four little children will one day live in a nation where they will not be judged by the color of their skin, but by the content of their character."[2] That day, a generation later, is much closer at hand—at least in the minds of many white and black children who know each other as friends because of their shared school experiences. The first time I discovered my son's second grade teacher was black was when I went for a parent conference, a month after school began. In all his descriptions of his teacher and his experiences with her,

Marc had never found her race worthy of mention. Indeed, I am not convinced he noticed it.

While moral education necessarily deals with the dilemma between what is right and what is wrong, sometimes (as in the case of Ellen's teacher) right is defined as being what the teacher says, wrong as being just the opposite. Actually, moral education is far more complex than training children to follow a set of rules or procedures. We are not after changing outward behavior so much as we are the beliefs of the heart. I can give up my seat to an elderly person because it is expected of me as the polite thing for a younger person to do; far better that I want to do so through my own inner sense of caring for another's needs.

Lawrence Kohlberg, Professor of Education at Harvard University, is today the most noted advocate of moral education in schools. He has expanded on the moral stages that both Dewey and Piaget helped define. John Dewey wrote that the "aim of education is growth or *development,* both intellectual and moral. Ethical and psychological principles can aid the school in the *greatest of all constructions—the building of a free and powerful character.*"[3] Jean Piaget contended that in developing morality, we must refrain from using rewards and punishments and instead encourage children to construct moral values for themselves.[4] For example, a child can learn honesty only if confronted with the fact that other people will not trust him or her unless he or she possesses that quality. Kohlberg applied both Dewey's and Piaget's studies to a solid, workable theory removed from religiosity but at the same time (and importantly for us) parallel to Christ's standard.

Basically, there are three levels which all of us as individuals go through in developing our moral characters. Level 1 is called the pre-moral, or preconventional, level. At this level, the individual feels no sense of obligation to rules unless those rules can do him some good or contribute to his personal gain (like punishment and reward, or an exchange of favors). Level 2 is conventional, or heteronomous, morality, meaning that the individual accepts with little critical reflection the standards of the peer group. The attitude is not only of conformity to the social order but of loyalty to it. Group identity is very strong at Level 2 and governs most behaviors. Indeed, while most people advance to this level, very few of us go beyond it.

Level 3 is the autonomous level—and intellectual and moral autonomy is what Piaget advocated should be education's major aim. Level 3 is characterized by behavior which is guided by the individual thinking and judging for himself whether a purpose is good. At this level, the individual does not accept the standard of the group without personal reflection. There is a clear effort to define moral values and principles that have validity and application apart from the authority of the groups or persons holding these principles and apart from the individual's own identification with these groups.

Kohlberg's major contribution to the current move back to moral education has been in setting up "Just Communities" that further define and refine these three levels into six stages, two at each level (though there is some feeling that perhaps it is not possible for any human to consistently function at the sixth stage; Kohlberg is adjusting his theory to span just five stages). These stages provide structures for moral judgment or reasoning as opposed to content.

It is not what is being decided on that matters but the process by which a decision governing action is reached. Do you run a red light when no police officer is around, but carefully stop when one is? Do you stop whether a police officer is in sight or not, because the law says to? Are there times in your life (being late to work, a family emergency, whatever) that you can justify running a red light, knowing full well that by doing so you put in peril the lives of people you may not know? The reason why you choose to stop or go—and not the act of stopping or going— is what determines the moral stage at which you are operating in making your choice. Judgment and reasoning matter more than content.

With this in mind, we can turn our attention to Kohlberg's six stages (understanding, of course, that the last has virtually

been eliminated as a consistent possibility for human achievement).[5]

Stage 1—The Punishment-and-Obedience Orientation: The
physical consequences of an action determine its goodness or
badness, regardless of the human meaning or value of these
consequences. Avoidance of punishment and unquestioning
deference to power are valued in their own right, not in terms of
respect for an underlying moral order supported by punishment
and authority (the latter being Stage 4). Ellen's teacher, functioning here, demonstrated his belief in the importance of this
lowest level of morality. Because of the impact of modeling, his
students could be expected to emulate him at Stage 1 as they
sought to "get along" in the world.

Stage 2—The Instrumental-Relativist Orientation: Right action consists of that which instrumentally satisfies one's own
needs and occasionally the needs of others. Human relations are
viewed in terms like those of the marketplace. Elements of fairness, of reciprocity, and of equal sharing are present, but they
are always interpreted in a physical, pragmatic way. Reciprocity
is a matter of "you scratch my back and I'll scratch yours," not
of loyalty, gratitude, or justice.

*Stage 3—The Interpersonal Concordance or "Good Boy-Nice
Girl" Orientation:* Good behavior is that which pleases or helps
others and is approved by them. There is much conformity to
stereotypical images of what is majority or "natural" behavior.
Behavior is frequently judged by intention—"he means well"
becomes important for the first time. One earns approval by
being "nice." Almost all of our schools implicitly teach this
stage of morality, though they do allow for some growth toward
the next one too. However, after Stage 4, there is little or no
opportunity in schools for moral growth.

Stage 4—The "Law and Order" Orientation: Authority,
fixed rules, and the maintenance of the social order are all
important at Stage 4. Right behavior consists of doing one's
duty, showing respect for authority, and maintaining the given
social order for its own sake. Peer pressure keeps most people

from moving beyond this level. Stage 4 rewards conformity to group norms. Aristotle wrote, "I have gained this by philosophy: that I do without being commanded what others do only from fear of the law." The law and order orientation does not allow for the inner impulse Aristotle wrote about. We obey because the law says to, not because we believe in what the law says. Soldiers in Nazi Germany who disclaimed responsibility for their own actions used supportive rationale that, at various times, moved them from Stage 1 to Stage 4, and then back again.

Stage 5—The Social-Contract, Legalistic Orientation, generally with utilitarian overtones: Right action tends to be defined in terms of general individual rights and standards which have been critically examined and agreed upon by the whole society. There is a clear awareness of the relativism of personal values and opinions and a corresponding emphasis upon procedural rules for reaching consensus. Aside from what is constitutionally and democratically agreed upon, the right is a matter of personal "values" and "opinion." The result is weight given to the "legal point of view," but with a stress upon the possibility of changing the law in terms of rational considerations of social utility (rather than freezing it at Stage 4's "law and order" orientation). Outside the legal realm, free agreement and contract is the binding element of obligation. This is, by the way, the "official" morality of the American government and constitution. It is not, however, that of most schools.

Stage 6—The Universal-Ethical-Principle Orientation: Right is defined by the decision of conscience in accord with self-chosen *ethical principles* appealing to logical comprehensiveness, universality, and consistency. These principles are abstract and ethical (e.g., the Golden Rule, God's categorical imperative); they are not concrete moral rules like the Ten Commandments. At heart, these are universal principles of *justice*, of the *reciprocity* and *equality* of human *rights*, and of respect for the dignity of human beings as *individual* persons.

Important to our study, Kohlberg believes Jesus Christ is the only human who ever behaved consistently at Stage 6. Mahatma Gandhi, Martin Luther King, Jr., and other important social activists operated at high moral levels, but primarily within Stage 5. People in Stage 5, for eminently worthwhile reasons, are out to change the law. But once the law is changed in favor of human justice, Stage 5 concerns often revert back to Stage 4—upholding the law because it is the law.

The Ten Commandments, in Kohlberg's view, essentially comprise a Stage 4 document. That is not the same as saying we obey them at a Stage 4 level. On the contrary, we may obey the Ten Commandments at a Stage 5 or 6 level. They are God's laws, yes, but at the higher moral stages they are upheld primarily because of a belief in their rightness, not out of fear of consequences for "breaking" them. The Golden Rule, on the other hand, is a Stage 6 admonition. In order to carry it out consistently, we would by necessity already have to be at the highest principled stage in our moral development. Indeed, if we all did to others what we wished them to do to us, no other law would be required for peace among people to be maintained. Because the Golden Rule is based on a principle rather than on a specific regulation, it can only be obeyed from the heart. There is no outward basis by which to confer compliance. It comes entirely from within.

It is also important to note, as Kohlberg does, that an individual is not necessarily operating at a high moral level just because he or she can understand all six developmental distinctions. Maturity and moral judgment have not been highly correlated with I.Q. or verbal intelligence. Instead of intelligence, the stage at which a person operates defines, first, *what* he or she finds valuable, and second, *why* he or she finds it valuable.

The universal issues of moral awareness affecting the concerns of all people are those related to punishment, property, roles and concerns of affection, roles and concerns of authority, law, life, liberty, distributive justice, truth, and sex. When two or more of these ten concerns are in conflict, a situation requiring choice is engaged. The individual is, at such moments, presented with a moral dilemma requiring personal decision. Which is more important, truth or life? Liberty or love?

A clarifying illustration cited by Kohlberg is found in the following conflict between property and life. A woman is dying. The inventor of the drug that could save her is selling it for ten times what it costs him to make it. The woman's husband cannot raise the money, and the seller refuses to lower the price or wait for payment. What should the husband do? He can choose between stealing, which morally he abhors, or he can watch his wife die, a choice he finds perhaps more difficult to contemplate. When an individual is confronted with a moral dilemma—with having to choose between two or more moral values, both or all of which are held dear—that individual's movement in the stages of moral development becomes clearer. It is our *reason* for choosing as we do that clarifies our level of moral thinking, and not our actual choice.

There are many possibilities here for teachers working with students in classrooms, which of course is what Kohlberg intended. As far as Jesus is concerned, he was himself continually presented with moral dilemmas by those intent on tricking him into breaking the law. Yet Jesus remained solidly a Stage 6 human being, with no law broken. And he did it by demonstrating the truth of Galileo's assertion that "facts which at first seem improbable will, even on scant explanation, drop the cloak which has hidden them and stand forth in naked and simple beauty."

Teaching Christianly: Do You Know the King?

"Brothers, have you found our king?" George Macdonald has demanded of us. "There he is, kissing little children and saying they are like God."

Indeed, finding Jesus is tantamount to finding our way as teachers of children. Jesus showed us how to exemplify to others the highest morality there is or ever could be. He did it by applying broad and solid principles of Christian behavior at specific moments when his veracity was under attack and when his knowledge of the law was severely questioned. We don't need specific methodologies and precise recipes for behaving if we understand his ethical principles.

Satan, of course, first put Christ to the test. "If you are the Son of God," Satan cajoled winningly, "then make stone into bread, or throw yourself down from that cliff so I can see the angels uplift you." It is tempting to show someone else "who's boss," to impress them with whatever powers and capabilities we have been given, and so it had to be for Jesus too. He was like us in all human ways.

But instead of succumbing to the temptation of proving once and for all that he was the Son of God, Jesus rebuked Satan. "It is also written, 'Do not put the Lord your God to the test'" (Matt. 4:7, Deut. 6:16, NIV). With these words, Christ answered the question of who he was and is, while refusing to be tempted into doing it on Satan's terms.

The Pharisees tested Jesus as well. Without giving credence to rumors of Jesus' divinity, they nonetheless asked him for a sign from heaven. Like Satan, they wanted him to declare himself openly as the Son of God. This was not because they longed to discern his true nature, but rather, because they wanted to entrap him into what to them would have been a blasphemous admission. Instead of being seduced by their plan, Jesus replied, "An evil and adulterous generation seeks after a sign; and a sign will not be given it, except the sign of Jonah" (Matt. 16:4, NASB).

By this Jesus meant that they would have to wait until the end of his life to see in his reference to Jonah a sign from heaven. Just as Jonah spent three days and nights effectively buried in the belly of a sea monster, so would Jesus be entombed in a grave for three days and nights before his resurrection. This, then, is the surest sign of Jesus' divinity, a sign he promised would be given and was. It is the convincement on which rests the doc trine of every disciple, the faith of every true believer, the courage of every martyr, the theme of every sermon, and the power of every evangelist. His answer may have seemed confusing then; it does not now. "The Lord God is subtle, but malicious he is not," Albert Einstein said with accuracy. Jesus does not play thoughtless tricks with our minds. His "sign of Jonah" answer is amazing in its simplicity and awesome in its fulfilled promise.

But the Pharisees sought to dupe Jesus in other ways as well. One one occasion they said to him, " 'Teacher . . . we know you are a man of integrity and that you teach the way of God in accordance with the truth. You aren't swayed by men, because you pay no attention to who they are. Tell us then, what is your opinion? Is it right to pay taxes to Caesar or not?' " (Matt. 22:16–17, NIV). If Jesus answered affirmatively, he would not be recognizing the supreme lordship of God. And if he answered negatively and mocked Roman law, the Pharisees would have been rid of the problem of Jesus. They knew that the Roman government would never tolerate a public denunciation of its authority.

Jesus recognized the hypocrisy in the moral dilemma put to him. The Pharisees did not want to know his opinion; they maliciously wanted to trap him into breaking the law, on one hand God's and on the other hand Rome's. They thought they had him in a "no win" situation. Either way, he was doomed—or so they thought. Jesus took into his hand the coin used for paying the tax, pointing out it had on it Caesar's portrait and inscription and not God's. He settled the issue by saying, " 'Give to Caesar what is Caesar's, and to God what is God's' " (Matt. 22:21, NIV). He operated by the highest of moral principles, recognizing infallibly what was important and what was not. He never broke the law, but neither did he obey it just because it was someone's idea of what the law should be.

In Mark we get this account: "One Sabbath Jesus was going through the grainfields, and as his disciples walked along, they began to pick some heads of grain. The Pharisees said to him, 'Look, why are they doing what is unlawful on the Sabbath?' " (Mark 2:23–24, NIV). It was, of course, unlawful to work on the

Sabbath. In many communities today it is still considered disrespectful, is not sacrilegious, to be seen working on Sunday. Work in modern terms is often defined as something like lawnmowing, and people's Christian commitment is frequently judged according to whether they perform such visible "working" acts or not. But Jesus' reply to the Pharisees is as revealing for us as it was for them: "The Sabbath was made for man, not man for the Sabbath" (Mark 2:27, NIV).

Another time he went into the synagogue, and again, "some of them were looking for a reason to accuse Jesus, so they watched him closely to see if he would heal [a man with a shriveled hand] on the Sabbath." Jesus asked them, " 'Which is lawful on the Sabbath: to do good or to do evil, to save life or to kill?' But they remained silent. He looked around at them in anger and, deeply distressed at their stubborn hearts, said to the man [with the shriveled hand], 'Stretch out your hand.' He stretched it out, and his hand was completely restored." Now, in the Pharisees' minds, Jesus had finally and irrevocably broken the law and scorned what they deemed important in the moral kingdom. So they "went out and began to plot with the Herodians how they might kill Jesus" (Mark 3:1–6, NIV).

Jesus infallibly knew what was important and what was not. Those of us today who are as convinced of the living God can do no less than help others interpret what is essential in life and what is not. This, however, has nothing to do with preaching or other outward shows of religiosity. Instead, it is based on modeling. It is toward this end—separating out the chaff from the grain—that God revealed himself through Christ. In most schools, and certainly in public schools, *our role as interpreters has nothing to do with public witnessing or direct preaching.* What it has to do with is instruction in how to relate to others in meaningful ways. It has to do with modeling the value of ethical principles and high moral standards.

Like Thomas Jefferson, an important framer of our Stage-5 American government, let us "swear, upon the altar of God, eternal hostility against every form of tyranny over the mind of

man." Having the power to make something appear more important than it is is certainly a form of tyranny, or mind-control.
We witness this in advertising all of the time. And not helping
young people's minds to grasp what truly is important is worse
than negligence. It is gross abdication of moral responsibility
and must not be countenanced in schools or anywhere.

The Past and Future: Active Instruction in Morality

It is important to look at a brief historical overview of morality as it has existed in American schools. It was out of the
context of the past that Kohlberg formulated his current the-
orizing about the pressing need for moral instruction in modern
schools. And Kohlberg and others lead us into the future where
considered instruction in moral principles must happen, and
happen soon.
Robert Frost wrote:

> Most of the change we think we see in life
> Is due to truths being in and out of favor.

The highest levels of morality never should go out of favor,
though they seemingly have. G. K. Chesterton said that "nothing sublimely artistic has ever arisen out of mere art, any more
than anything essentially reasonable has ever arisen out of pure
reason. There must always be a rich *moral* soil for any great
aesthetic growth" (italics mine).[6]
In colonial times the primary purpose of formal education was
to enable people to read the Bible and to improve their moral
status. For decades moral improvement continued to be *the*
purpose of education. After the Revolutionary War, the goal of
an "informed citizenry" was added to the purposes of education. For a democracy to succeed, it was thought that citizens
needed to be moral and informed. According to most current
practices in education, "informed" seems now to stand alone as
the overriding educational goal of our time.

Two factors contributed to the decline of the direct teaching of morality in schools. The first was the application to education of the principle of separation of church and state. This was not always an educational imperative, as it is today. Actually, it was designed to be a governmental imperative to protect religious freedom and not, as is supposed, to provide freedom from religion. John Marshall warned, "The people made the Constitution, and the people can unmake it." Perhaps we are in the process of doing that very thing.

The second factor contributing to the decline of direct teaching of morality in schools was skepticism about the effectiveness of it. Studies showed that the addition of morality, ethics, and religion to classroom curriculum did not prevent children from lying, stealing, and cheating. Thus, direct moral instruction fell to a low point by the 1950s because it was believed to do little good.

Nevertheless, the Gallup Poll of 1980 indicates parents have a renewed interest in "zeroing in" on moral education in contemporary classrooms. Eighty percent responded positively to the question, "Would you favor or oppose instruction in the schools that deals with morals and moral behavior?"[7] Several indicators point to the reason behind this renewal of interest: the narcissistic-hedonistic trend in our society; rising divorce, crime, delinquency, and illegitimacy rates; the alienation of the young; cynicism regarding involvement in civic affairs; and the deception and self-seeking of elected officials. "Millions pass through the educational system," wrote Alvin Toffler in *Future Shock*, "without once having been forced to search out the contradictions in their own values systems, to probe their own life goals deeply, or even to discuss these matters candidly with adults and peers."[8]

Yet, alongside of these important concerns, there is also a positive trend toward active participation in religions, student activism in the face of injustice, a greater number of adolescents who engage in community welfare activities like the Big Brother/Big Sister organization, and who contribute their efforts to charities and serve at camps such as those run for victims of muscular dystrophy. In general, adolescents are doing more than their bad press would seem to indicate to provide encour- agement in several different ways to others less fortunate than themselves. Teachers find that children of all ages can readily be made aware of the need for acceptance of, and friendship to, handicapped or culturally different youngsters.

Glen Heathers says there must be a new set of psychological requirements for living in the future. Among the aims that should receive emphasis in our educational programs to meet these future psychological requirements is an involvement of all students in community study and participation in community activities.[9]

This school-in-community approach should provide for reg- ular interaction with both formal and informal community agencies and organizations. Also included as another aim is the understanding and appreciation of people and cultures else- where in the world, with emphasis on industrially less-devel- oped countries in Africa, the Middle East, Asia, and South America. Stress should be placed on teaching the process by which individuals grow from infancy to adulthood in different societies, using data obtained from cultural anthropologists. Our understanding of and appreciation for world-wide diver- sity will be greatly enhanced by such classroom undertakings.

Moral education—distinguishing right from wrong as a Stage 5 or Stage 6 person would—is implicit in Heathers' psychologi- cally secure approach to the future.

Childhood's Security: Knowing Right from Wrong

The cover picture on Urie Bronfenbrenner's book, *Two Worlds of Childhood: U.S. and U.S.S.R.,*[10] betrays the gist of his revealing study. It shows two small families, one Russian and one American, each with a mother and father and a child in tow. The Russian couple is carefully and protectively cradling their child in their arms while holding their nation's flag

proudly over their shoulders. The American couple, on the
other hand, has their child dangling loosely and carelessly from
their fingers. They are holding the American flag upright by
their waists, but it is a listless and awkward act without depic-
tion of national pride.

Bronfenbrenner's book deals with the topic of the socialization of children in both countries. In the Soviet Union, not only
is there deep maternal nurturing of children, there is society-
wide nurturing as well. That is, small children are revered and
affectionately played with by even complete strangers. They are
kept from harm's way in playgrounds and on subways and buses
and wherever strangers encounter other people's children. Physical demonstrativeness is the norm, being very much in evidence
and widespread in practice. The Russians love their children,
and thus, hold teachers of young children in highest esteem.
Collective parenting and educating is carried out through both
formal and informal means at all levels of their society.

The Soviets are doing some things so well, in fact, that we
would do well to study their procedures. They seem to be applying Western research to their own particular political system
better than Western countries are to theirs. An example is their
stress on *vospitanie,* which is loosely translated as meaning
"character education." While we are relegating the education
of moral character to those forces found outside of our schools—
namely, the family and the church—the Soviets embrace just
the opposite tact and grant *vospitanie* the highest place in their
school system. Bronfenbrenner terms our way the "fateful separation of church and state, which, as it freed the schools of
religious control, also fragmented the process of education."
Bronfenbrenner also calls this the "unmaking of the American
child."

Children are being unmade, according to Bronfenbrenner,
because "parents have become powerless as forces in the lives of
their children." Children in our country used to be brought up
by their parents, but the fact that they no longer are is not
necessarily the fault of the parents. Indeed, far from not caring,

most parents today are more worried about their children than they have ever been in the course of recent history. Bronfenbrenner cites as the crux of the problem "a society which imposes pressures and priorities that allow neither time nor place for meaningful activities and relations between children and adults, which downgrades the role of parents and the functions of parenthood, and which prevents the parent from doing things he wants to do as a guide, friend, and companion to his children." We are in the process, Bronfenbrenner warns, of experiencing a breakdown in making human beings human, and not only that, our schools have become one of the most potent breeding grounds of alienation in American society.

William Golding's *Lord of the Flies* gives us a frightening view into a lawless society run by displaced children. All manner of violence, including murder, has erupted among a group of boys marooned on an island. Sadism, dictated by peer pressure, quickly becomes peer power. The first question the adult rescuers ask upon finding the boys is, significantly, "Are there any adults—any grown-ups with you?"[11] The unspoken answer is, of course, no. Bronfenbrenner concludes that the "message of the allegorical ending is clear and . . . dictated no less by literary insight than the independent data of behavioral science. If adults do not once again become involved in the lives of children, there is trouble ahead for American society."

Bronfenbrenner's study of these two contrasting cultures shows us surprising and terrifying things but ends on a note of hope: "For just as autonomy and aggression have their roots in the American tradition, so have neighborliness, civic concern, and devotion to young. It is to these that we must look if we are to rediscover our moral identity as a society and as a nation." Moral identity involves knowing the difference between right and wrong. Having a clear-cut moral code gives security to childhood. It answers imponderables, providing direction and purpose to actions and activities. Without it, life looms as a meaningless vacuum. All too many children—and adults, as well—know the insecurity of feeling caught in purposelessness.

Psychologist Bruno Bettelheim, who believes in the importance of fairy tales to children's lives with their clearly right/
clearly wrong imagery, writes that "the child must be helped to
make some coherent sense out of the turmoil of his feelings. He
needs ideas on how to bring his inner house into order, and on
that basis be able to create order in his life. He needs . . . a moral
education which subtly, and by implication only, conveys to
him the advantages of moral behavior."[12]

Choice of Climate: External Control vs. Self-Discipline

The Phi Delta Kappa Commission on Discipline defines the
goal of school discipline programs as "to teach students to behave properly without direct supervision."[13] In this is Piaget's
belief that autonomy is what is most important in establishing a
climate of true learning. When opportunities to achieve moral
autonomy are not provided, students typically react with a
backlash of confusion and alienation. Demonstrably "out of
control" themselves, they perceive how much better it would be
to be "in control," to be the "power figure" that their teacher is.
A desire to be powerful is not uncommon among alienated
children. It might exhibit itself outside the classroom, perhaps
through bullying on the playground or through some other form
of equally assertive and antisocial behavior. It might exhibit
itself inside the classroom in actual attempts to wrest control of
the class from the teacher. William Glasser writes, "Many
teachers are desperately searching for an alternative to the
power struggles that so often contaminate their teaching."[14]
But calling for autonomy in no way implies that every child
should be allowed "to do" his or her "own thing." Usually that
results in classroom chaos.
What, then, is the answer to achieving behavior in classrooms that is socially acceptable?
As one response to this, a number of philosophers, psychologists, and physical educators eulogize sports, believing games
develop morality and socialization in children through the real-

ities of playing and winning and losing. Self-discipline is thought to evolve from participation in sports. Excess energy is given an outlet, and so, children's disciplinary infractions are soothed through physicality.

With the advent of "pee wee" leagues—conducted along the lines of the major leagues in football, baseball, and soccer—it seems, instead, that increasing numbers of kids are turned off and burned out through participation in these highly competitive contests. Children who watch adult models (in particular, their parents and coaches) are learning how to swear, cheat, fight, and deride the umpire. Psychologist David Elkind calls these little leagues "the worst destroyers of the playfulness of sport."[15] Sports writer John Underwood chimes in with agreement. "[Coaches] make eight-year-olds sit on the bench while others play, learning nothing beyond the elitism of win-at-all-costs sport," he says. "Token participation—an inning in right field, a couple of minutes in the fourth quarter—can be equally demoralizing."[16]

Obviously youth sports programs have the potential for facilitating moral development when conducted correctly. Incorrectly, they can produce amoral and immoral behavior. Very few of them, unfortunately, retain their playfulness. In most, small children are dressed up in expensive uniforms and pressured to win.

Some who believe that participation in sports isn't the total answer to instilling self-discipline in children postulate a reward and punishment approach to solving classroom behavior problems. Currently, a program called "Assertive Discipline" is achieving widespread popularity in our nation's schools. This plan calls for rewarding (stars, happy-grams to parents, and so forth) "good" behavior and for punishing (name on board, deprivation of privileges, calls to parents, and the like) "bad" behavior.

The problem with "Assertive Discipline" and its kin is really threefold. Because such plans give clearcut rules and put students on notice when they break the rules, it becomes the student's or principal's responsibility to find a way to correct the underlying problem. What happens on the outside, and not the internal reason behind inappropriate behavior, is the focus. This absolves teachers of the responsibility to be caring, mature persons with some degree of autonomy in their classrooms. Individual needs of children are not taken into account. Indeed, doing so would be seen as inconsistent and, therefore, unacceptable to running a smooth "show."

A second problem exists in this reward-and-punishment approach to disciplining. Justice is sometimes not meted out under such a plan because extenuating circumstances are of no importance to the plan. In fact, having definite answers for every occasion is what is attractive about it to many teachers. Through elimination of all "gray areas," penalties and rewards are sometimes given to students who don't deserve either. Let's look at how this happens.

Perhaps the rule is never to be late to class, yet here comes a tardy student. Suppose the student who is late has stopped along the way to help a fellow student retrieve and wipe off homework papers accidentally dropped in a puddle. Is it fair to be punished for helping someone in need? Where is the moral teaching in that? Regarding reward, perhaps the first student who arrives in the classroom—and the one who, by earliest arrival, will be designated as "teacher's helper"—is only first because he or she shoved three people out of the way in order to get through the door first.

Individual or extenuating circumstances have to matter. There is a legitimate plea in our court system, which is called "Guilty, with explanation." I know. I used it once after receiving a traffic ticket. I couldn't argue that I wasn't going forty miles per hour in a thirty zone, as the police officer said I was. Because I was deliberately doing exactly that, on the face of it I deserved the ticket. But I could argue *why* I was traveling at that speed. And, as it happened, the judge understood and accepted my explanation. In view of my extenuating circumstances, I was not punished with the full fine. And I was content with the judge's fairness in looking at my problem's individuality.

Finally, and maybe most important, assertive discipline contains no provision for teaching students to behave properly without direct supervision—the most important goal of any school discipline program. It is reliant on a controlling adult's influence at all times.

A third way of approaching the problem of classroom discipline is utilizing what could legitimately be called the "nagging method" because of its resemblance to incessant scolding. In practice, if not theory, this may be used by more teachers than any other technique. It is a technique characterized by carping. We demand exemplary performance of children often without explanation of *why* such performance is judged exemplary. We enforce compliance to our standards via strength of our position and status. We are the parent, or we are the teacher, and that seems quite enough reason to expect our demands to be met. When a child asks, "Why do I have to do that?" we in effect reply, "Because I said so."

This is not always bad. In fact, I warrant it is sometimes even necessary. But overdone it poses dangers for our children's moral development. What it really teaches is that "might makes right." It teaches that it is all right to "bully" another if you are stronger than they are. It awakens a lust for power, for power's sake. It alienates those who are not within the power structure. "If only," a child thinks, "*I* could be the one whose word is law! Wait till that day comes. I'll be boss then!" And it, like assertive discipline, leaves some doubt as to whether the behavior being sought will continue after the nagger has left the child's presence. Sometimes a backlash, held in check until the nagger disappears, will occur instead. But our apparent belief in the benefits of nagging exemplifies again the "outside-in" approach to much of our teaching. In effect, this type of teaching assumes that if external behavior is controlled, a child will automatically internalize the behavior's "superiority" and will continue to exhibit such behavior in other situations. There is no convinc-ing proof that this is so.

A fourth approach, one that has gained in popularity through recent years, is that of value clarification. Because we live in an era of changing values, value clarification has helped bring a good deal of talk to classrooms regarding the importance of those things which ultimately contribute to happiness. On the positive side, this approach has given students experience in thinking critically about their values and has given them oppor-tunities to share their perceptions with others. It has even helped them learn to apply valuing processes to their own lives, seen as an important aid for ultimately achieving self-knowl-edge, and thus, self-discipline.

It has *not* (and I believe this to be a highly significant omis-sion) allowed teachers to take any moral stand. In fact, value clarification exercises are characterized by moral neutrality. Im-plicit in them is the notion that all values are equally valid. Therefore, no clear standards of right and wrong prevail in classrooms where teachers undertake this approach. And if no clear standards prevail, insecurity most assuredly will.

A fifth approach could be called the "liberal arts" approach. In this is the idea that if a person reads widely, thinks deeply, and experiences broadly from a curriculum based on our rich and diversified cultural heritage, moral truths will emerge. Tra-ditional values and beliefs are the cornerstone of a liberal arts approach. Censorship of ideas is not allowed, because it is be-lieved that only exposure to any number of differing ideas will create understanding of what is right and just and honest. In it is contained the definition for becoming fully educated and fully human.

Mortimer Adler's *Paideia Proposal,* which advocates a broad liberal arts education for everyone ("paideia" is the Greek word for general human learning), contains much of this philosophy. One of the main tenets of the proposal is that a liberal course of study *must* include three kinds of learning: acquisition of orga-nized knowledge, development of the intellectual skills of learning, and an enlarged understanding of ideas and values. "These three kinds of learning and the corresponding three kinds of teaching," Adler insists, "must be integrally related to one another."[17] Moral development and character building are vital to true education.

Even in 1657, John Amos Comenius wrote about how to become more human. His thoughts, like the concepts in the *Paideia Proposal*, centered on an education which embraced the humanities:

> The education that I propose includes all that is proper for a man, and it is one in which all men who are born into this world should share. Our first wish is that all men be educated fully to full humanity. Not any one individual, not a few, or even many, but all men, together and singly, young and old, rich and poor, of high and lowly birth, men and women; in a word, all whose fate it is to be born human beings, so that at last the whole of the human race become educated, men of all ages, all conditions, both sexes, and all nations.[18]

An education in the humanities is not "what's left over when you finish with the sciences." The word "humanities," Dr. Adler tells us, is "strictly the equivalent of *paideia,* which means general, unspecialized, untechnical human learning." In fact, he also says that "liberal arts are not fine arts. The fine arts are totally useless; that is their glory. The liberal arts are useful . . . reading, writing, speaking, listening, and all the mathematical arts and scientific skills. Those are the liberal arts. They are skills. Arts are skills." And Adler and proponents of *paideia* see those skills contributing to a unifying morality through their internalization.

The National Commission on Excellence in Education report, *A Nation At Risk: The Imperative for Educational Reform,* says at one point to parents, "You know that you cannot confidently launch your children into today's world *unless they are of strong character* and well-educated in the use of language, science, and mathematics" (italics mine).[19] Moral development is essential to the well-being of our nation, as well as to the orderly climate of our individual classrooms.

As they were in the mind that meticulously reasoned through the path toward life, liberty, and the pursuit of happiness, Thomas Jefferson's thoughts continue to be relevant to teachers and students seeking answers for peaceful co-existence. "I know no safe depository of the ultimate powers of the society but the people themselves," Jefferson wrote, "and if we think them not enlightened enough to exercise their control with a wholesome discretion, the remedy is not to take it from them but to inform their discretion."[20]

What does all this imply for us? I cannot say it better than Harold Shane did, writing for the *Phi Delta Kappan*. His recommendations from 1976's "America's Next 25 Years: Some Implications for Education" are well-summarized by Callahan and Clark in *Introduction to American Education*:

> You must first begin to think in terms of providing a model of decency and thoughtfulness for young learners.
>
> Second, you and the rest of the teaching profession must work diligently to build inner security in children and youth insofar as this is possible, because inner security is the best armament for life in an insecure world.
>
> Third, all of us citizens must consider seriously a renewal of belief in the value of rules to live by: guidelines inferred, in considerable measure, from our concern for a threatened biosphere and from an understanding of what serves humanity's long-term well-being.
>
> Fourth, we teachers must help our young people develop the courage to live with uncertainty and a service ethic which is geared to the real world. This includes the morality of conserving, recycling, creating as much as we use, as well as establishing a dynamic equilibrium between humans and their myriad environments.
>
> Fifth, implicit in this concept are the moral insights that will help us live with the regulated freedom we must eventually learn to impose upon ourselves in a world characterized by increasing dynamic reciprocity.[21]

In self-imposed discipline, or self-discipline, there is freedom. What is the purpose of discipline if not freedom? Isn't that what morality is all about—achieving freedom for every human individual? Certainly that is the intent of the Golden Rule. The danger in focusing on outward behavior instead of inward motivation is that outward behavior then becomes the end in itself, as if outward behavior is what self-discipline is all about. Through that screen nothing is seen but rigid, inflexible rules. All we have achieved is legalism, and we don't have to look very far in public education to see where teaching outward behavior has taken precedence over helping instill inner discipline. "The moment we make [discipline] our central focus," Richard Foster writes in *Celebration of Discipline*, "we will turn it into law and lose the corresponding freedom."[22]

Moral Implementation: Some Ideas

If we look once again at the three basic moral levels, focusing on examples of behavior at each level may help us to see how we can help young people grow toward more advanced moral reasoning.

The first level—the concern for external, concrete consequences to self—is exemplified through the title of a book, *Pray and Grow Rich* (Ponder, 1968). This level of morality is connected to a "let's make a deal" syndrome, and even the title of this book reflects its moral mentality. It advocates striking a hedonistic bargain with God. If you pray (or obey God), he will reward you by making you rich. If you scratch God's back, he'll in turn scratch yours.

Another example is provided by Karmel and Karmel: "People often say, 'I can't believe in a God that would allow deformed children to be born.' Translated, this means: 'Why should I scratch God's back by believing in him when he won't scratch my back by preventing unpleasant things from happening in the world?'"[23] Such reasoning reflects the bottom of the three levels of moral development.

Most people advance to the second level of moral functioning. This is the level of the good, law-abiding citizen. People
operating here may feel a law is unjust or inequitable (such as a
natural mother's "right" to reclaim her already-adopted child),
but they will support or uphold the mother in court because the
law is the law. Children and adults who are at this level of
conventional morality are apt to go along with the crowd. A
teen-age boy may get "talked into" a night of beer-drinking with
a group of friends, followed perhaps by shoplifting or robbery at
an available convenience store, though he would engage in none
of these acts if he were alone. A young woman might become
enmeshed in a gossip session about an absent friend, even
though she recognizes some of the things being said are unkind
and untrue. She may keep silent or nod agreement or even add a
choice comment herself. These are all characteristics of the middle level of moral development, in which concerns for meeting
external social expectations have the foremost internal ranking.

The highest, or third, level is characterized by self-accepted
moral principles. At this level, there is primarily a concern for
fidelity to *chosen* standards. The individual has examined the
roles, social conventions, and laws of society, but he or she has
reached a reasoned conclusion on the rightness or wrongness of
these issues for him or herself. Internalized convictions are all-
important, based on what is just, generous, sympathetic, and
understanding of others. These, of course, are the principles
upon which a democratic society is based. Karmel and Karmel
point out that in a "judicial system based on flexible morality,
there is room for mercy. Although there are many faults to be
found in such a judicial system, it is constructed so that the
intention of the person who committed the crime enters into the
judgment."[24]

It was at this level that Corrie ten Boom and her family could
disobey the "law of the land" and hide Jews in their home. It
was at this level that they could risk incarceration and death in a
concentration camp for their actions. It was at this level that
both Mahatma Gandhi and Martin Luther King, Jr., could ad-

vocate civil disobedience—or deliberate ignoring of the "law of the land"—in order to obey a higher principle. Perhaps not many of us will reach the status of the individuals mentioned, but in countless ways we are each given opportunities to choose among the principles of justice and equality and those of lesser importance.

In working with children, we who are adult care-givers must provide times of moral discussion. The school environment it-self provides many such opportunities. Recall with me the ten universal issues of moral concern which, when in conflict with each other, present moral dilemmas to people: punishment, property, roles and concerns of affection, roles and concerns of authority, law, life, liberty, distributive justice, truth, and sex. Ask students, Which is more important, your need to take home a passing grade on your report card (punishment) or my right to know it's your own work that earned it (truth)? Which is more important, finishing your homework on time (authority) or going to the movies with your friends (affection)? Which is more important, an opportunity for a date with the girl or guy of your dreams (sex) or a visit to your hospitalized, gravely ill grandmother (life and/or affection)? On and on, moral dilemmas are available for classroom discussion. And always the *why* of a choice must be examined. It is the reason behind a decision, and not the decision itself, that is at the heart of moral functioning.

The Phi Delta Kappa Commission on Discipline found five factors to be necessary for creating an environment that encour-ages teachers and students to feel good about themselves and that develops and maintains a culture conducive to learning. These five factors are:

1. Creating student belongingness and responsibility.
2. Pursuing superordinate school goals.
3. Creating symbols of identity and excellence.
4. Fostering leadership to sustain positive school values.
5. Creating clear formal and informal rules.[25]

Used in tandem with one another, these basic ideas produce an inviting school environment. It is an environment which, through structured curricular means, helps develop self-discipline. Indeed, a school must undertake to implement specific "agenda items" if it is truly interested in instilling both moral values and acceptable social behavior.

There, of course, has always been a hidden curriculum in schools—that is, the subtle ways that teachers and other adult authorities transmit moral lessons to children—but it is time now to make character development an active component of daily classroom life. In a country designed as ours is, we are constantly called upon as citizens to reach common understandings on complex issues, often on short notice and often on the basis of conflicting or incomplete evidence. This requires moral nurturing and higher-order thinking skills in line with a developing awareness of internal principles of "conscience" and respect for the rights, life, and dignity of all persons. Moral principles have universal validity. That is, they are the same for all persons. They are not the exclusive domain of those proposing one religious persuasion or another. Likewise, laws governing behaviors should be derived from morality, and not the other way around. "The best use of laws," Wendell Phillips said, "is to teach men to trample bad laws under their feet."

Perhaps the divinely inspired wisdom of Martin Luther on instilling moral values deserves the last word. "What can only be taught by the rod and with blows," he said, "will not lead to much good; they will not remain pious any longer than the rod is behind them." Children have a desperate need for teachers who care for something far richer than outward bendings to someone else's will. Children have a desperate need for teachers who help seek moral solutions to life's many complex dilemmas. Indeed, children have a desperate need for interpreters of what is important to know about living.

CHAPTER SEVEN

Do Teachers Really Like to Come to School with Kids?

THE NEED FOR LEARNERS

"You ought to see that bird from here,"
said Rabbit. "Unless it's a fish."
"It isn't a fish, it's a bird," said Piglet.
"So it is," said Rabbit.
"Is it a starling or a blackbird?" said Pooh.
"That's the whole question," said Rabbit.
"Is it a blackbird or a starling?"

—A. A. Milne—

Making ourselves into lifelong learners may be the most important aspect of any teaching. Authentic teachers are authentic learners. But "learning is not attained by chance," Abigail Adams warned, "it must be sought for with ardor and attended with diligence." Teachers must consciously cultivate their zest for learning. It is a prime requirement for undertaking the job. "He was a bold man who first ate an oyster," Jonathan Swift observed; teachers, too, must be characterized by boldness. Without apology they must be willing to boldly assert, "I don't know everything, but I'm open to learning." Only then can they truly begin to teach.

My eleven-year-old son once taught a university class of prospective teachers. During his fifth grade year, he was involved in a fascinating World War II study project which had him doing such non-textbook assignments as actually meeting a Jewish survivor from a Nazi concentration camp and speaking via telephone with Maria von Trapp—whose wartime escape from the Nazis was made famous in *The Sound of Music*. On one occasion, he and his classmates experienced prejudice and fascism firsthand by losing their recess if they had blue eyes. On another occasion, those who wore jeans to school were given the right to "boss" everyone who wasn't wearing jeans. And the first hour of each day throughout the project, all students were required to sit stiffly in their desks, feet flat, hands folded, eyes forward, and to stand at attention in the aisles for both the asking or answering of questions.

The mastermind behind this enormous project was a teacher who continually strove to involve her students in an array of books, films, and maps, always incorporating exercises like journal-writing that required personal investment to complete. The children, with unparalleled eagerness, explored their innermost depths as they attempted to understand exactly what it was humans endured in World War II. Very few people forty years removed from a historical event have crawled back inside it the way this class of fifth graders did.

The final "test" for this project was to spend a morning at a neighboring university, fielding questions from college students enrolled in both undergraduate and graduate teacher education courses. The questions ranged from the particulars of how the project was designed to what the children actually learned to the remarkable depth of their feelings for the victims of Nazi oppression. And the victims, these children discovered, included people fighting a confusing and confused war, no matter which side they represented. Sometimes, these students saw, people victimize themselves and suffer for a lifetime by their willingness to "go along" with moral aberration. Yet the children's exposure to injustice, while filled with painful conclusions, contained only the scantest sense of condemnation, if even that.

My son was a panelist in one of the university classrooms, and I sat unobtrusively in back, watching it all. As the audience warmed up, questions were fired at the panel. The children's "performance" did not fail to amaze everyone in that room, including some previously skeptical prospective teachers who otherwise never would have believed ten- and eleven-year-old kids were capable of such depth and perception. The college students experienced role reversal that day. For a time the adults were the learners, and the children were the teachers. The fifth grade teacher herself assures anyone who will listen— and I believe it—that she was a student of the children's insights throughout the entire project. Teaching and being taught had merged.

Models for Study: A Peek at Some Great Learners

We can be better learners than we are. In fact, if we are to effectively teach, it is essential. Some of the greatest minds the world has known were not always of that quality. Those individuals helped bring about their own "greatness" through careful attention to self-development. A look at them and at what they accomplished through a commitment to improve themselves can help us.

Mahatma Gandhi was one such individual. In *The Life of Mahatma Gandhi,* Louis Fischer writes: "Ideas came to [Gandhi] occasionally through books but chiefly through his own acts. He remade himself by tapping his own inner resources." Gandhi's education was desultory and Hindu in character. "It is not," his biographer asserts, "that he turned failure into success. Using the clay that was there he turned himself into another person."[1]

Gandhi enjoyed reading the Old Testament's prophets, as well as Psalms and Ecclesiastes. Even more, he enjoyed the New Testament and found, in particular, that the Sermon on the Mount (in Gandhi's own words) "went straight to my heart." Next to Hinduism, he was most attracted by Christianity. He loved Jesus. "Hindu bigots," Fischer writes, "even accused him of being a secret Christian." It has been said that the great sin of those claiming Christ will always be that brotherhood was not extended to Mahatma Gandhi. Instead, the Christian world deliberately shunned him, even refusing him access to its churches. So when no one would teach him about Christ, Gandhi taught himself.

Booker T. Washington was another individual who rose from inauspicious beginnings to become one of the foremost educators and reformers of all time. He was born in a slave hut. The dire poverty of his family ruled out any opportunity for regular schooling. By age nine, Booker T. Washington was working in a salt furnace. Later, his youthful toil took him to a coal mine. Yet he was determined to become educated.

Eventually, through desire and force of will, he became a teacher. Around the clock he taught, children by day and adults by night. Among his many altruistic accomplishments was the development of a successful educational program for American Indians and, most importantly, the founding and nurturing of the Tuskegee Institute. Tuskegee stands today as a monument to Booker T. Washington's lifelong goal, that of providing higher education for people who otherwise would be prevented from attaining it.

A third lifelong student worthy of attention was Abraham Lincoln. Lincoln, a gifted man, had little formal schooling. While there are several legends about his so-called "studying into the night by the light of a single candle" and about his "tramping miles through snow to return a book he'd borrowed," the fact still remains: Lincoln epitomizes the self-taught human. Not only was he a student of his own teaching, he was a student of human nature. His observations of people are both wry and perceptive. They are also tinged with gentleness and overriding compassion. Surely his ability always to be slightly amused by life kept his sanity intact as he carried the most excruciating burdens any American chief executive has ever known. There is a lesson in Lincoln's humorous approach.

But the larger lesson is in Lincoln's continued zest to know and understand, to call on the best from himself even when others actually discouraged that best from surfacing. Had his scholarship been reliant on external imposition, it is doubtful we would still be a nation. If Lincoln had not "taught himself," he would never have grown as an individual and been prepared to lead us from the abyss of civil strife. And throughout his White House years, not the least of Lincoln's legacies to us (as Elton Trueblood has ably chronicled)[2] was his theological maturation.

It was himself and God that Lincoln sought to satisfy. In the face of overwhelming pressure and criticism, Lincoln could observe, "It is difficult to make a man miserable while he feels he is worthy of himself and claims kindred to the great God who made him." He epitomized Aristotle's assessment that "to enjoy the things we ought and to hate the things we ought has the greatest bearing on excellence of character." Yet in his crude beginnings and in his lack of formal education and material resources, and indeed in his famous "homely" visage, Lincoln represents all of us. "The Lord prefers common-looking people," he once said. "That is why he makes so many of them." He saw people at their worst and continued to like and believe in them. In spite of all he endured, he could ask, "Why should there not be a patient confidence in the ultimate justice of the people? Is there any better or equal hope in the world?" Lincoln was a consummate pursuer of higher understanding.

Thomas Jefferson put the concept of ultimate justice in a slightly different context. "Indeed," he said, "I tremble for my country when I reflect that God is just." Jefferson, though different in wealth, shared many characteristics in common with Lincoln. Like Lincoln, he was fascinated with learning. His mind was active and grew increasingly more brilliant because of his own careful nurturing of it. He was one of the most extraordinarily learned men of recent times, a feat made more remarkable because most of his learning was self-imposed. His interests in the arts and sciences were wide ranging, highly complex, and amazingly inventive. Jefferson's insatiability as a human being was in his quest to know and, thereby, to grow. His personal library at Monticello was one of the largest in the world during his lifetime.

But he did not limit his educational pursuits to just a desire for his own growth. He coveted the experience on behalf of everyone. While several of America's founding fathers expressed belief in the necessity of public education, only Thomas Jefferson undertook to translate his conviction into actuality. Convinced that democracy could only be effective in the hands of an enlightened people, Jefferson devised a plan for his native Virginia that called for the education of all children at public cost.

Jefferson met strong resistance to his plan, and it came from the ruling class, who said education should be the domain of those who could afford it, and from the clergy, who said education of the "common man" was the responsibility of the church hierarchy. Jefferson's educationally philanthropic dream has still not been fully realized. Indeed, it took forty years for any portion of his plan to be put into place during his own lifetime. The development and creation of the University of Virginia, which students still call "Mr. Jefferson's University," is today the only tangible evidence of Thomas Jefferson's personal impact on making a liberal education available to all.

From across the world comes another example of learning, and of teaching. One of the foremost philosophers of all time, Immanuel Kant, by birth a Prussian, was first and foremost a popular and lively teacher. Philosophy came to Kant as a secondary interest, and the writings for which he is known came still later. Besides the more traditional lecturing in physics and mathematics Kant did throughout the academic year, every summer for thirty years Kant offered a course in physical geography. It was always immensely successful, enrolling a diverse population of students eager for the experience of studying under him. Kant's teaching style, which differed markedly from the more scholarly discourse found in his books, was humorous and vivid, enlivened by many examples lifted from his vast reading in English and French literature, and from travel and geography, science and philosophy.

Kant refused prestigious positions at other institutions, including a professorship of poetry at Berlin, preferring instead the peace and quiet and contemplative lifestyle found in his own native city, Königsberg. Amazingly, almost all of Kant's major writings occurred between his seventieth and eightieth birthdays. His mind was nurtured for a lifetime by his own interest in learning. He never lost his curiosity. After his death at age eighty, his tomb was inscribed in German with words he himself wrote: "Two things fill the mind with ever-increasing wonder and awe, the more often and the more intensely the mind of thought is drawn to them: the starry heavens above me and the moral law within me."

A noteworthy female contemporary of Jefferson's and Kant's was Sacajawea. Sacajawea's story is a fascinating one. Crossing racial, sexual, and cultural barriers that would seem to preclude the opportunity to have a lasting impact, Sacajawea has had more memorials raised in her honor than any woman in North American history. She became famous for leading the Lewis and Clark Expedition (commissioned, coincidentally, by then-President Thomas Jefferson) through thousands of raw wilderness miles to the Pacific Northwest. And, during the entire trip, she carried her infant son on her back.

Sacajawea (called "Janey" by Captain Clark) was a Shoshone woman of immense courage and fortitude. At the age of twelve, she had been sold into slavery. A French-Canadian fur trader, who was later to become Lewis and Clark's interpreter, eventually bought Sacajawea. It was her connection to this man that allowed Sacajawea the opportunity to serve as Lewis and Clark's guide through the vast, unexplored Indian territory.

She performed brilliantly in the face of hardships and deprivations which we can barely begin to imagine from the comfort of the 1980s. Yet she was, except for her own alive mind, unschooled in any formal sense. She called on her own strength of will and inner resources and, from that formidable mental depth, resolutely helped forge our nation. Although historians have trouble sorting out the legend from the reality of Saca- jawea, enough is known about her actual life to make her a worthy example of what it is possible to do, if only the desire to learn how to do it is there. Indeed, the very fact that exaggera- tion has arisen around her life and incredible deeds contributes to her stature. Unremarkable people do not inspire legends.

But perhaps one of the most surprising examples of commit- ment to learning comes from the life of Jesus Christ. Jesus, the most infallible human being the world has ever known, a person who would appear to need no learning, engaged himself in ex- actly that. "Although he was a son," the writer of Hebrews tells us, "*he learned obedience from what he suffered*" (Heb. 5:8, NIV, italics mine). Our principal Model models not only learning, he models a lifelong commitment to it. Learning obedience did not come easily or all at once, not even for Christ.

Like Jesus and other great learners, we need to be students as well as teachers if we hope to accomplish what we must. If it was important for Christ to receive instruction, how much more important is it for us? We are, each one of us, still in our infancy as earthly teachers.

Revisiting Childhood: Teaching's Unique Fringe Benefit

Infancy has its benefits. Through staying close to youth in spirit, there is much we can learn. The opportunity to revisit childhood is one of teaching's most attractive fringe benefits. In it is contained the chance to retain freshness in our quest for learning. The opportunity to revisit childhood may even be a fringe benefit *unique* to teaching. What other job has a daily dose of insights readily provided by thirty-plus "teachers"? Adult care-givers have as their main task being open to perceiv- ing interactions with children for what they are: moments to learn from some of the most inventive minds God has created. Good minds must not go to waste on us. Children are God's messengers—and sometimes God's mirrors.

From a toddler in a high chair, who has begun understanding her mother will not let her eat food that has fallen on the floor, comes the act of deliberately dropping food when she doesn't want to eat it.

From a three-year-old who places his hand over his pregnant mother's distended abdomen and feels the inversion of her navel comes the excited cry, "Mommy, I can feel the baby's toe!"

From a five-year-old, who lives in Wichita, Kansas, a new interpretation of the Pledge of Allegiance is produced: "I pledge allegiance to the flag of the United States of America, and to the public of Wichita . . . " And from another comes the demand to know what it is under God that is invisible.

From a seven-year-old involved in contemplating his expanding world originates this thoughtful observation: "Mom, I know why they didn't call schools 'helicopters.' "

"Why?"

"Because if they did it wouldn't make any sense."

A child in a Sunday school asks what made Jesus cross-eyed. The startled teacher asks why she thinks he is, to which the child replies, "Because we sing, 'Onward Christian soldiers, marching as to war, with the cross-eyed Jesus, going on before.' "

Another child terms fingertips that have just finished washing dishes, "my shriveled little babies." Still another likens envy to "a monkey looking at me through the bars of his cage." And from a high school student trying to cope with life's manifest uncertainties come these funny, poignant lines:

> Oh, great cheetah, you are so fast
> Have ever you felt the embarrassment of last?

One student-poet wrote, "Kindness is a puppy licking my sore toe." Children's needs, or their "sore toes," become apparent when we open ourselves to listening to them. Their insights become apparent too. Through them we learn re-sensitization, such as that of forgiveness and compassionate mercy. A young Anne Frank, who did not live beyond childhood, can amaze us by confiding to her diary, "In spite of everything I still believe that people are really good at heart."[3] Or we can learn the quality of love and the release of humor. One Mother's Day, from my son whose favorite food is a legend around our house, came a homemade card which contained a simple but (to me) eloquent statement, "I love you more than macaroni and cheese."

Dick Van Dyke tells the story of the student who defined "democracy" as "that system of government where one man is as good as the next, and sometimes a lot better." Children are citizens of the second type.

The learner in each of us must always be alive and well and receptive to instruction from even the unlikeliest of sources. The only thing "unlikely" about children as potential teachers is our own inability to take them seriously. This is where genuine caring enters in. We must care for our students deeply and truly. They must be authentic human beings to us, or we will not open ourselves to what they have to teach us. Children can provide something unique to our lives.

Caring: Its Relation to Learning

We learn best from people we care about. In order to truly care for students, teachers must find the person in each one of them. Sharing names is a good way to begin doing this. Find out how your students acquired their names and tell them how you acquired yours. Questioning may be a helpful beginning. Is it a family name? If so, which person in your family did it first belong to? Does your last name have a meaning? What nationality did it originate from?

It is important to get "inside" students in other ways, too (and these techniques work with students of any age, and in any type of teaching situation, preschool to college, public schools, private schools, and even Sunday schools). Ask such things as, Do you have any well-known relatives? What is a favorite story your grandmother told you from her childhood? If you could ask one of your long-ago relatives anything you wanted, what would it be? What is the most interesting thing you have ever done, the most interesting place you have ever visited? What is your earliest memory? What were you doing last year on this date? What do you want to be doing next year on this date? What was your favorite (or least favorite) birthday? If you could choose the date of your birthday, when would it be?

The ways of gaining insights into students' personal lives are endless and, ultimately, *very* important to a teacher's enjoyment of being with them. Seeing students as humans, as truly separate and individual people and not just as a collection of animate objects who happen to be sitting in chairs in the same room, will help a teacher's (and parent's) job remain eminently more interesting. Acknowledging the particularity of another is a strong expression of love.

Indeed, caring is essential to the teaching/learning process. But it is not enough. In *On Caring,* Milton Mayeroff provides a wise caution against over-reliance on love:

> We sometimes speak as if caring did not require knowledge, as if caring for someone, for example, were simply a matter of good intentions or warm regard. But in order to care I must understand the other's needs and I must be able to respond properly to them, and clearly good intentions do not guarantee this. To care for someone, I must *know* many things. I must know, for example, who the other is, what his powers and limitations are, what his needs are, and what is conducive to his growth; I must know how to respond to his needs, and what my own powers and limitations are.[4]

This kind of knowledge comes neither easily nor all at once. There is a constant, pressing need for up-dating and revitalization of our understandings of basic interpersonal principles if we are to work effectively with children. One course as an under-graduate in a teacher education program will not fulfill this imperative, even though it may be all that technically is "required." From somewhere within each of us must come an internal commitment to continued pursuit of new insights, no matter what our degree programs impose on us. If we are not able to "call upon" ourselves in this manner, we will never become the teachers we can and must be.

Mindless Fads: Fashion's Big Business

In speaking of learning or self-development, the specter of "self-help" looms. Indeed, self-help books flood the market-place. Money is made by dispensing wisdom on the power of positive thinking and on motivating the growth of inner re-sources. Without a doubt, God has given each of us more inner potential than any of us will utilize in a lifetime.

These self-help mechanisms are not necessarily bad as we struggle to attain personal growth, but of more importance than these or anything else purporting to deliver condensed wisdom is a guiding philosophy of life. Fads in whatever guise are still that: fads. Our culture puts tremendous pressures on us to be "with it." For good reason a fad is often called "a craze." Obviously something concrete must be available to us—such as commitment to an overriding philosophy—in order for us to weather the storms a deluge of conflicting fads present us in a lifetime.

Our culture is currently caught up in the fitness fad. It could aptly be termed a "get-in-shape craze." People who don't spend time on Nautilus machines and in mixed aerobics, who don't wear fashionable sweatsuits and color-coordinated leotard out-fits, are thought to be out of touch with society's current "guid-ing light"—body toning via trendy health clubs. Most commu-nities, in fact, have so many of these clubs that they drive each other out of business in competitive urges to be ever more attrac-tive and appealing. An observer of health club promotion could gain the impression that these places are filled with clinking wine glasses and chandeliers—signs of the "good life"—instead of the gritty smell of sweat.

From a health perspective, fitness makes excellent sense. In fact, good health requirements demand proper care of our bodies. But do these requirements necessarily demand where and how the act of staying in shape occurs? A guiding philosophy of life helps sort such issues out for us.

Principles are important here, not specifics. Specifics can be faddish. What people do must not become more important than why they do it. In *Love, Acceptance, and Forgiveness: Equipping the Church to Be Truly Christian in a Non-Christian World,* the promotion of private Christian schooling as a solution to the problem of the quality of education and the moral climate in public schools is challenged by the authors. That solution, it is pointed out, "does nothing to help the public school. To the contrary, removing the Christians tends to abandon the public school system to its doom."[5]

By no means am I attempting to imply that opting for a private education is inherently wrong. Sometimes it may be the best—or even only—alternative in sight. But what must be guarded against is allowing such a choice to become faddish or trendy, without having behind it the considered weight of thoughtful introspection. Why are we opting for one way of educating children, and rejecting another? It is a very important question.

Mindlessness' Redemption: A Guiding Philosophy

A philosophy evolves into a plan of action only after the action planned is examined through the magnifying glass of basic beliefs. The United Methodist Church, for one, has taken a denominational position of committing itself universally to the support and betterment of public education. No private Methodist elementary and secondary schools exist. But there is nothing about living by this plan or any other that is easy or that lends itself to the fickle whims of fashion. Criticism and doubt are always waiting to attack those who exercise the considerable power of their minds.

Responsible teachers who want to grow in their professionalism must actively seek to understand where they themselves stand on matters related to the basic humanities—the humanities being defined as general, unspecialized, untechnical human learning. Knowing where you stand philosophically regarding something as basic as learning is the answer to why theory is every bit as important in colleges of education as is classroom methodology. No one is capable of functioning consistently without a theoretical undergirding.

Without a base, we are all, the adult care-givers of us, in danger of exploiting the sin of "mindlessness," surely one of the most wicked evils that could befall school curriculums anywhere. Whether it is founded on public precepts or private ones, no type of school can do its job in an atmosphere of mindlessness. Each teacher behavior, no matter how minute or inconsequential it might appear, must be based on a guiding philosophy—and be defensible according to that philosophy's basic beliefs.

In *The Teacher as Philosopher,* Douglas Simpson and Michael J. B. Jackson point out the distorted picture caused by misunderstanding the practical activities of the teacher on one hand and the theoretical issues on the other. Theory, they say, need not be impractical. "A theory, after all, is a theory about something, and in practical matters people do act for a reason or have something in mind which makes sense of their choices."[6] Or, shall we say, people ought.

By studying and being learners themselves, by pursuing personal development through immersion in deep thought and not by skimming the surface of intellectual history, "teachers, like anyone," Simpson and Jackson tell us, "develop more fully as human beings. . . ." Teachers have human needs requiring satisfaction that are independent of their societal status as teachers. Through yearning toward wisdom, "by coming to recognize themselves and their activities, by coming to theorize about themselves and their world, including their role as teachers . . . the study of philosophy helps the teacher to become more fully *homo sapiens,* 'the one who thinks.' "7 It may be self-evident and overly trite; nevertheless, we need the reminder that mind-lessness can only exist where thinking does not.

"Burnout": Causes and Preventatives

If we do not develop ourselves as human learners, there are serious dangers awaiting us. Archibald Hart, the Dean of the Graduate School of Psychology at Fuller Theological Seminary, looks at burnout in *Coping with Depression in the Ministry and Other Helping Professions.*8 It is a revealing book for ministers and others, like teachers, who work closely and intensively with human beings. " 'Burnout,' " Dr. Hart warns, "is a phe-nomenon that is increasingly becoming a serious problem among . . . [those] in the helping professions." While this is not to suggest that everyone involved in a profession like teaching will experience symptoms of burnout, neither must we be blind-ed to its possibility.

Indeed, the type of teaching I am proposing makes more de-mands on an individual and is, through doing so, more likely to contribute to burnout. Devotion to learning, on the other hand, can help prevent it. We shall look briefly at what burnout is and what its causes are before we move on to an examination of the importance of learning in its prevention.

Why are those who work closely and intensively with human beings—such as doctors, nurses, counselors, social workers, ministers, and teachers—more apt than those in other profes-sions to experience burnout? Probably because working with diverse personalities, by its very nature, brings with it a built-in source of frustration. Burnout is the result of prolonged de-bilitating stress. The balance between need satisfaction and frustration has tipped, as Carducci and Carducci say, "toward frustration too often over too long a period of time. Burnout is a

form of depression."9 Symptoms are fatigue, anxiety, irri-
tability, headache, appetite and sleep disturbance, loss of feelings of self-worth, loss of goals or optimism about reaching
them, loss of confidence, anger or rage, impulsiveness, tear-
fulness, and even physical illness.

Teachers must continue their own individual development
long after the formal requirements leading to certification are
behind them. Keeping interested in life is a vital ingredient in
prevention of burnout. Most states have implemented recer-
tification plans which require teachers to complete additional
college coursework after a period of years. However, an internalized impetus to achieving this end is always more beneficial
than is one that is externally enforced. It is important that
teachers strive to keep alive their knowledge of and commitment to the psychological and communicative principles of
healthy interaction. Revitalization is continually necessary for
all people in the helping professions. Caring teachers are not
fearful of admitting their need for continued growth. They
don't have all the answers, and they're not reluctant to say so,
though this is not the same thing as self-flagellation, or recount-
ing one's weaknesses over and over to others.

In *On Being a Christian,* noted theologian Hans Küng
observes:

> To many a non-Christian it seems that the Christian is so intent
> on self-denial and self-renunciation that he neglects his self-devel-
> opment. The Christian may indeed want to live for men, but he is
> often not enough of a man himself. He is very ready to save others,
> but he has never learned properly to swim himself. . . . He is trou-
> bled about the souls of others, but does not recognize the complexes
> of his own psyche. By attaching too much importance to and mak-
> ing too many demands on love of neighbor, service, self-sacrifice, he
> is very likely to break down, become discouraged and frustrated.
>
> In fact is it not the failure to be fully human which so often makes
> being a Christian seem inadequate? . . . Must we not strive for the
> best possible development of the individual: a humanization of the
> whole person in all his dimensions, including instinct and feeling?

Being human ought to be complementary to being a Christian. The Christian factor must be made effective, not at the expense of the human, but for the benefit of the latter.[10]

For some Christian teachers there is a double conflict over how best to deal with their own humanness. They serve in an authoritative capacity where children look up to them for instruction and guidance. It isn't considered "professional" to be "too human." Archibald Hart says, "I have found that many . . . Christian leaders have a haunting suspicion that they are hypocrites. . . . [But] if we are going to avoid unnecessary depression we must learn how to turn failure into growth and to become courageous in facing our imperfections." Or, in Alexander Pope's words, "A man should never be ashamed to own he has been in the wrong, which is but saying, in other words, that he is wiser than he was yesterday."

Facing ourselves in our full human glory (even though to us it may seem less than glorious), coupled with accepting what we see, is one of the best preventatives against burnout. As a friend of mine said, "Let's face it: I'm not O.K., you're not O.K., and that's O.K.—because we live under grace." Through acceptance of ourselves, we let loose of the burden to live by a set of impossible expectations. Instead, we can begin living to accomplish God's will through recognizably transient flesh. This is important in establishing the basic attitude we form about ourselves and others, an attitude that we will inevitably carry with us into our jobs.

In searching for young people to include in leadership seminars he helps sponsor all across the nation, Hugh O'Brian writes to high school principals to ask for their help in identifying fifteen- and sixteen-year-old potential future leaders:

I'm looking for high school sophomores who have leadership potential and are concerned about tomorrow. Perhaps the boy or girl who won the election to Class President comes to mind first, but what about the youngster who ran for the office and lost? What did that person learn that the winner didn't? What kinds of strengths did the experience melt into that student's character that will over-come obstacles yet to be faced?

Facing our failures honestly is a way to turn those failures into re-sensitized growth. Failing is another way of learning. As it was with Christ, suffering is the school for learning obedience to God. Albert Einstein was labeled a backward student, and Thomas Edison was thought to be apathetic toward education. In their early years, they were not among the "elected." Being among the elected—especially if to be so is an end in itself—does not always guarantee growth. In fact, it usually prevents it.

Renewal: Becoming Students of Our Own Teaching

If we are in danger of burning out, we must be aware of how to stay on fire. Educator Herbert Kohl has discovered an in-teresting paradox: "First, many teachers are tired and demor-alized and, second, despite this mood there is more creative teaching going on than there has been in years." In other words, many teachers are learning how to creatively overcome the insidious specter of burnout. We need to examine their secrets.

In his book *Insight: The Substance and Rewards of Teaching,* Kohl gives us a glimpse of one teacher's philosophy: "My salary doesn't keep up with inflation," Kohl quotes this teacher as saying. "The papers and magazines blame me for everything negative that happens. I don't know whether I'll still have a job next year or whether I'll be shifted around somewhere in the district. If I can't have some pleasure in the classroom and take some risks to teach, well, I might as well quit and drive a cab or something."[11]

To relieve stresses over which they can exercise little control, many teachers are deciding to have "fun" with their teaching. And they carry out this decision, or implement risks, in any number of interesting ways. Such teachers guard against directly or indirectly "buying into" Kohl's satirical "Ten Reasons Why I Can't Teach Well This Year":

1. The administrators won't let me.
2. There isn't enough money to buy the new program I want.
3. The students aren't motivated.
4. The climate isn't ripe for change.
5. I tried that before and it didn't work.
6. All that parents care about are the basic skills.
7. Because there are too many students in my class I can't be creative.
8. I don't have enough time to plan.
9. The materials I need aren't on the approved list.
10. Nobody will appreciate what I do anyway.[12]

Teachers who care about staying alive and vital—and who are aware of the pitfalls if they don't—look for topics which interest them personally and which they can, then, continue to pursue away from the job. They don't always read and study just what is directly related to their classroom preparation. They might go in-depth in personal study time with a topic that is beyond their students' comprehension, but which was introduced or touched on originally in interaction with children.

In other words, our own classrooms can provide the catalyst for discovering new interests. Teachers who are open to this happening might take a college course related to the area of interest, or form a discussion group with similarly interested people—perhaps with colleagues on the faculty, or with a group of church friends. Such individuals are effectively functioning as students of their own teaching.

Some teachers concoct surprises for students which are carefully planned ahead; others improvise on the spot in order to delight and provide adventure for both themselves and their students. Either way, a teacher's interest in classroom happenings is kept alive and aglow.

An example of someone who concocted a surprise is Lewis, a

teacher with a pilot's license and a passion for flying. Lewis, during the course of beginning a new school year, recognized the special needs of Dirk, a boy in his junior high classroom. Dirk's needs, to Lewis's practiced eye, seemed similar to his own. Dirk drew pictures of airplanes all over his notebook paper, but was lax about filling those pages with anything more closely aligned to the subject matter. Lewis hoped to provide Dirk with a unique motivation to do better.

Making arrangements "on the sly" with Dirk's parents—who obligingly kept Lewis's plan secret from their son—Lewis, with a show of nonchalance, called Dirk over to him after school one day, threw his arm around Dirk's shoulder, and said, "You want to go flying?" And "go flying" they did. An immediate trip to the airport and a climb into the aircraft Lewis regularly used (privately, he'd dubbed it "The Spirit of St. Lewis") was all the preparation Dirk was given to experience the thrill of a lifetime. His relationship to his teacher was solidified in such a way that Dirk never again wanted to disappoint Lewis. And the "spontaneity" of their flight together was just as much fun for Lewis as it was for Dirk, lending a feeling of renewal to both of their efforts at school.

An example of the second type of spontaneity—the improvised on-the-spot kind—is shown by Pat. Pat teaches second grade. One March, a student in Pat's room spied a robin pecking along the brown earth outside the classroom window. Since it was the first robin most of the children had seen that year, its appearance created quite a stir. Spring was coming! Pat decided to seize the moment and turn it into a science lesson.

"What is the robin doing?" Pat asked.

"Looking for food," chorused the children.

"But what food? I don't see much to eat out there, do you?" The children fell silent. They didn't see much either.

Issuing a spontaneous instructional invitation, Pat then asked, "Shall we go out and see if we can find what that robin has found?"

So on went the jackets and out went the class. They explored the seemingly bare ground carefully. Through spring detective work, they discovered bits of greenery emerging from the soil, a few insects crawling in the dirt, scattered seeds, and so forth. In a word, they found what the robin had been looking for. But until the robin was seen outside the window, the spring exploration had not been part of Pat's classroom plans. She improvised the lesson on the spot. By allowing herself this crucial bit of flexibility, both she and her students had a fun, memorable day. Opportunities for teaching and learning are important in Pat's classroom.

There is a veritable smorgasbord of choices available to teachers for keeping classrooms alive and well. Among them is the importance of providing a place to which the *teacher* wants to go, as much as do the kids. Plants, attractive bulletin board displays, neatness and order should permeate an atmosphere that is welcoming to all its inhabitants. Just as our own homes show us, daily environment has a large impact on our emotional well-being. Pleasantness begets pleasantness.

Humor, as well, is an essential ingredient in preventing classrooms from becoming oppressive. Humor in no way should be thought to mean having an arsenal of stand-up comic routines and hilarious jokes ready for delivery. Indeed, most of us would not qualify for teaching if that were the case. No, humor is best exemplified through a pervasive lightness of touch, through seeing things as funny rather than wrong. A measure of graceful wryness often can be a teacher's best friend in defusing potential discipline problems. While laughing at others is not to be tolerated, an outlook containing playful amusement and a bent toward jocularity is an excellent weapon against the defeatism so often caused by human conflict.

Learning simple tools of relaxation is another guard against burnout. Developing a quiet time is more and more essential in our frenetic world. Surely during the traditional nine months of a school year, no one is more frenzied than good teachers. Closing their eyes and counting to push away intrusive thoughts, relaxing their bodies one part at a time from the toes on up, visualizing themselves someplace special and soothing—like at the seashore or mountains or in a featherbed—are techniques many people find helpful. And, of course, Christians must not overlook the essential daily need for a meditative time with God.

God offers the ultimate peace for our busy souls. A skilled psychotherapist himself, Archibald Hart nevertheless writes with conviction, "It is my strong belief that Christian conversion has saved more people from ruination, suicide, drug addiction, alcoholism, resentment, and anger than any system of psychiatric or psychological treatment I know."[13] That is not to say that once a person accepts Christ, all problems disappear. Every mature Christian knows otherwise. But it is to say that with that acceptance of Christ comes a very powerful Healer and Friend, an Intercessor of the first order into the problems of the world. For mental and emotional wholeness, it is essential in our daily lives to not lose touch with him.

Peter Ustinov has said, "I am convinced it is of primordial importance to learn more every year than the year before. After all, what is education but a process by which a person begins to learn how to learn?"[14] An eloquent echo of the same thought comes from poet Richard Purdy Wilbur in *For Dudley*:

> All that we do
> Is touched with ocean, yet we remain
> On the shore of what we know.

Teachers must not neglect caring about such a determining concept as being a student first, a teacher second. Making ourselves into lifelong learners is not only important to us as teachers. It is important to us as human beings. Indeed, it may be the most important ingredient for reaching those levels of human maturity that are within our finite grasp.

CHAPTER EIGHT

What Are You Doing the Rest of Your Life?

THE NEED FOR COMMITMENT

"Cheshire-Puss," said Alice, "would you tell me,
please, which way I ought to go from here?"
"That depends a good deal on where you want to
get to," said the Cat.

—Lewis Carroll—

Commentator Paul Harvey's book, *The Rest of the Story,* reveals an ironic incident in the life of Edwin Thomas Booth. Edwin, like his better-known brother, John Wilkes Booth, was an actor. In truth, Edwin was a more gifted actor than John, but his talent, tragically, was always obscured by John's infamy. Some critics maintain that Edwin's quiet, introspective style of act-ing—largely due to the agony of being indirectly associated with the Lincoln assassination—inspired the move toward the theatrical realism of the twentieth century. At any rate, Edwin Thomas Booth had perhaps an even more remarkable impact on history than that, though at the time it occurred he did not know it.

One evening Edwin was waiting on a platform to board a train. Suddenly, without warning, the coach he was about to enter lurched forward. To his dismay, Edwin saw a well-dressed young man fall near the tracks, pinned between the platform and the moving train. Quickly and reflexively, Edwin wound himself around the guard-rail and grabbed onto the boy, pulling him back to safety. The young man recognized his rescuer as the famous actor, and shaking Edwin's hand, thanked him warmly.

Edwin went on about his business, not knowing who he had saved. It was only later with the arrival of a thank-you letter from Washington that Edwin was informed of the identity of the young man. In Paul Harvey's words, "It was as though by some terrible tipping of the scales that Edwin had spared the son of his brother's victim. While one brother had killed the President, the other had saved the life of the President's son . . . Robert Todd Lincoln."[1] Edwin Thomas Booth carried that bittersweet letter of thanks to his grave. It was found in his pocket at his death.

Making Choices: Salary and Other Big Benefits

Sometimes we don't make choices. Sometimes, it seems, they are made for us. Edwin Thomas Booth, while inheriting his brother's "name," could still, in an unplanned moment, be available to save rather than take the life of a Lincoln. He could right some of the wrongs, behaving better than what others expected of him. Such times of spontaneous decision seem to find us, too, whether we consciously seek them or not. And, afterwards, we won't always know where the waves that ripple out from such "choices" lead. Indeed, it is likely we never will.

Along with Hans Christian Andersen, we yearn to hear the song of the nightingale, a sweet song that warms our hearts and stills our fears. "The little live nightingale . . . had come to sing of comfort and hope. As he sang, the phantoms grew pale, and still more pale, and the blood flowed quicker and quicker. . . . Even Death listened, and said, 'Go on, little nightingale, go on.'" Teaching can be like that. I promise you it can. It can be that way for you, and it can be that way for the students you teach. Long after you are gone from their lives your students will continue to hear the "song" you sang for them.

Having this kind of enduring, dynamic relationship with students is one of the important plusses for choosing teaching as a career. When asked what their personal and professional motivations were for pursuing studies to become teachers, some of my college students replied thoughtfully and introspectively.

I have found that my principal motivation comes from my spiritual life. If I let it wander or collect a little dust, it shows in the rest of my life, physically, emotionally, and mentally. As a result, that will always be my number one priority. Teaching will help keep my spiritual life alive. I want my students to see me and know what I am modeling. I had hoped to teach in a Christian school, but after my teacher assistance experience, I have decided I should be in public schools.—Susan

I really want to be an elementary school teacher. I know I couldn't help but enjoy teaching children because they're so interesting. I like to see how they think and how they react to different things. . . . Also, I've learned that it is very important to be doing something self-satisfying (and not in material terms).—Jennifer

My future plans are quite simply laid out: I plan on continuing my education and on working to become a good teacher. I am quiet and a little on the shy side, but sometimes I can be outgoing and even 'radical.' Personally, I'm glad that I do have different sides to me because that way I can be flexible. Flexibility is important in teaching.—Don

The people in my life that have affected me the most are my parents. They are both teachers. They have convinced me that education is important to the rest of a person's life—and that education never stops.—Guy

At this point in my preparation for my career, I am many things. I am, to name just a few, both bold and shy, confident and confused, and excited and nervous. . . . One minute I can be tongue-tied and awkward, the next a clown hogging the limelight. It's as easy for me to be childish as it is for me to be mature and sophisticated. Who knows? That may never change. But I'm pleased with my life as I envision it. I see many opportunities opening up to me. As I continue to grow, I know 'the Lord is my strength and my song.' — Tracy

When I first began my teacher assistantship experience at the junior high, all those kids could do was stare at me. 'Who is that big guy?' they'd ask their instructors. . . . The instructors told me to open up to the kids, to 'break the ice,' so to speak. That was one of the best suggestions I've ever had in my life. After that, it was a whole new learning experience for me. I got to see how the kids thought and what they thought. . . . Now the most important thing in my life is to get my degree so I can teach.—Ben

None of these college students mentioned the material rewards of teaching as being important to their choice of teaching as a career. Actually, since teachers' salaries are notoriously low when compared to educationally and experientially similar jobs, by necessity a special kind of person is attracted to the teaching profession. It must be a person whose main goal in life is not to grow wealthy in material terms. Assuming we follow Christ's example, service occupations, rather than those designated to "make" money, are worthy of serious consideration. Teaching fits into this category. Indeed, through teaching's service orientation, Christians are eminently, perhaps even uniquely, suited to the job.

Research on outstanding teachers, whether professing Christians or not, indicates their decision to teach comes from a love of learning, a sense of mission, and a desire to work with people. Most teachers graduate from their college training programs with idealism and an almost naive commitment to making an

immense and discernible difference in classrooms. Somewhere
along the way, many of them lose this initial fervor. Perhaps
they discover that, if they make a difference, it is by no means
discernible.

There is danger awaiting children when their teachers' idealism erodes. If teachers do not actively seek to recapture their
sense of purpose despite classroom realities (such as its very
"dailiness"), they will become burned-out shells of their former
eager selves, entrapped by unhappiness and encircled with
failure. True, many of these individuals victimize themselves,
but more important, they victimize students who cannot learn
ideals if their teachers have none.

On-the-Job Doubting: Satan's "Diminisher"

I used to believe there was no such creature as a devil incarnate, or literal devil. Instead, Satan to me was personified
through the potential for evil lying dormant in all of us. Sometimes it awakened and—boom!—human horror erupted.

I no longer believe that. I now believe through personal experience with his wiles that Satan strikes me repeatedly and ear-
nestly, and that he does so in those areas where I am weakest
because of natural disposition. He is real, he is insidious and
deceptive, and he knows me well.

Actually, it is common for most teachers to go through periods of self-doubt. It has been, and is, for me, too. Taking those
normal periods of "on-the-job doubting," as I call them, and
twisting them around in our minds, making them huge and
overwhelming, is one of Satan's favorite tactics against sincere
teachers. Perhaps less sincere teachers are less susceptible to
severe doubts—perhaps such teachers are even characterized
by unwavering confidence—because they are less damaging to
Satan's overall purpose, which is of course the destruction of
God's plan for human beings. Satan will leave those teachers
alone if they are not primarily concerned with enacting God's
will. Granted, they may be secondarily concerned with God—
they may even be active Christians—but if *primarily* they are

concerned with justifying or defending themselves in the class-room, or in having their own needs met, these people are not of particular interest to Satan. Indeed, he sees them as posing little threat to his ends.

All teachers go through a natural evolutionary cycle. Teaching is developmental by its very nature. And because doubting and discouragement are part of the normal process of growing as a teacher, Satan can count on their occurrence. He will be waiting to take us at those moments, which is to say during our greatest vulnerability to him, and make more of our feelings than they are. Consequently, we must be alert. If we understand the cycle, we will be better able to maintain our acuity when we most need it.

As researcher Katherine Newman discovered, there are five basic stages along a teacher's trek through her or his career.[2] The first can be called, "Initiating the Career." At this beginning stage, a teacher is just emerging. A college student graduates and accepts a contract for his or her first teaching assignment. These beginning few years are spent learning how to teach (university programs cannot tell you everything—don't ever expect that they will). The first few years are also spent in a struggle for survival. The necessity for expenditure of high energy is frequently accompanied by periods of complete exhaustion. Discouragement and depression are not uncommon, particularly if this stage is not recognized for what it is—a *learning* stage. Preparation for the job, in some sense, is just beginning when a college graduate receives a degree certifying him or her to teach. It is a time of adventurous new beginnings, not endings. (College graduation is called "commencement.") Only now is God sending you on your ministry, if you are a new teacher. Remember, Jesus' steps did not get easier during that point in his life. In fact, Satan tempted him sorely (we can be sure we'll be tempted too), but Jesus did not lose his idealism. Instead, he solidified it, and so can we.

The second stage is called by some, "The First Decade." It is at this stage that a teacher switches levels, schools, or subject matter to find her or his niche in the system. This is also a time

for re-evaluation. A decision may be made to leave teaching—
for which there must be no sense of shame—or to take time off
to start a family, or to go back to college to "bone up" in certain
areas and explore specialized interests, or perhaps this will even
be the time to begin a totally different career. In my favorite of
her many marvelous books, *Tuck Everlasting,* Natalie Babbitt
has a wise old character advise us:

> Everything's a wheel, turning and turning, never stopping. The
> frogs is part of it, and the bugs, and the fish, and the wood thrush,
> too. And people. But never the same ones. Always coming in new,
> always growing and changing, and always moving on. That's the
> way it's supposed to be. That's the way it *is.*[3]

It is all right for teachers to "move on." It is all right for them
to find other niches, either in the profession (which we will talk
about in a moment) or out of the profession. In either case, if
they have been guided by the principles we have already discussed, such teachers will have contributed more to students'
lives than most other people ever will. They should not consider
themselves failures. Length of time is not a criterion. I have seen
some teachers teach not twenty years, but the same year twenty
times. I have seen others accomplish miracles with only a few
months on the job. Good teaching is not based on endurance.
Rather, it is based on commitment to certain important guiding
principles. As long as adherence to those principles stays fresh,
so will teaching. But when it has disappeared, so should the
teacher.

The third stage can be labeled, "Satisfaction and Stability." It
is at this level that a person achieves a certain status in the
classroom and in the schooling organization. Now that the
teacher has moved through the first decade, he or she should be
teaching the desired subject at the preferred grade level. However, there is a caution which must be observed at Stage 3.
While a sense of satisfaction prevails, a loss of energy and increase in fatigue is likely. Most people in their thirties or forties

(the most common ages for reaching this plateau) are not necessarily thrilled to be already doing what they can expect to be
doing the rest of their lives, no matter how satisfying their
labors are.

This reality leads us into the fourth stage, or the "What's It
All About?" stage. Here a person ponders life, career, and retirement benefits. It may be a time of questioning and recommit-
ment. Actually, a change within the educational community
may be necessary. It could be time to move to administration,
perhaps a principalship, or to undertake school counseling or
another specialty of some sort. Perhaps it is time to apply for that
coveted "department head" position or to be considered for the
honorific title, "master teacher"—a movement in some districts
which I wholeheartedly endorse. It is the psyche, more than the
pocketbook, that is in need of a raise in "pay."

The fifth and last stage is, "When to Retire?" It is here that a
person faces the reality of approaching retirement. Questions
about whether it all was worth it may surface. The children of
earlier students may begin to appear in class, as well as other
signals of "career age." Decisions must be made regarding the
propitious timing for a graceful exit from the profession.

So, all excellent, Christ-centered teachers, be alert: Satan
wants you discouraged. He wants your effectiveness wiped
away. Knowledge of these stages—and knowledge of Satan's
active presence in the classrooms of authentically Christian
teachers—should help guard you against taking normal on-the-
job doubting too seriously.

Good Teachers: Glimpsing the Faces of Christ

Poet Carl Sandburg wrote, "The Christ head, the Christ face,
what man will ever paint, chisel or carve it? When finished, it
would float and gleam, cry and laugh with every face born
human. And how," he asked, "can you crowd all the tragic and
comic faces of mankind into one face?"[4]

Sandburg's insight is exactly what makes teaching such a

difficult profession. Teachers, through the people-demands of their jobs, must keep attempting to discover how to "cry and laugh with every face born human."

Jesus was a teacher. In fact, he was *the* teacher. Some personal characteristics of those who effectively teach in the manner of Christ are: *empathy,* or accurately perceiving what students are experiencing and then communicating that perception; *respect,* or displaying deep and genuine appreciation for the worth of students; *genuineness,* or being freely and sincerely oneself (exhibiting nonphoniness); *warmth,* or making positive comments of concern and affection for students; *concreteness,* or exploring the what, why, when, where, and how of students' experiences; *confrontation,* or detecting and reflecting to students discrepancies between what they say and do, including discrepancies between what they communicate verbally and what they communicate nonverbally; *self-disclosure,* or exposing one's own thoughts, ideas, feelings, experiences, and attitudes at a crucial time for the benefit of students; *immediacy,* or encouraging students to deal with the here and now in a realistic way; and *potency,* or communicating command of oneself, which elicits feelings of security, safety, and trust from students.

Some of the prospective teachers with whom I work, in reflecting back on their elementary and high school years, discovered several of their former teachers who exemplified all or most of these characteristics. In these examples are found people who help us see more clearly the "faces of Christ."

In searching for a prototype from her childhood years, one student told me, "I don't know of any specific teacher who doesn't have faults as well as good qualities." Her comment helps us realize our human shortcomings in ever being *as* Christ—and how some of us fall way short. "However," Denise went on to say, "there is one teacher that I would consider above the others. He was my high school band director." During Denise's senior year in high school, a new vocal music teacher was hired. The new teacher had a difficult time learning to relate to students. He was insecure in his job, and it showed.

The students grew contemptuous of his insecurity. Their dislike took on burgeoning proportions, until the band director interceded. With characteristic gentleness, he reminded Denise and her classmates that the vocal instructor was "a new teacher and needs your patience and support or he will never be able to grow in the way you want him to." Furthermore, he said, "you should have seen me fifteen years ago. I'm grateful that the students I had then gave me a chance."

Denise now gladly admits, "My band director was a good scholastic teacher. I learned lots of music theory from him. But he also taught me something about respecting other people in each situation. By just observing him and his life, I learned what it means to really be fair."

Another student, Dana, away at a Christian boarding school for many years, remembers a math teacher who was "not only a friend, a mother away from home, and a counselor, but a professional. She knew what she was teaching, and she was confident not only in herself but in her students as well." One incident Dana particularly recalls is that this teacher telephoned each student at home prior to the trigonometry and calculus final exam to offer to set up a special conference in her office, if the student had any questions spanning the material to be tested. Only after this favorite teacher's death did her students discover that she suffered from a chronic liver disease that was quickly killing her. None of them saw her daily pain.

Kevin fondly remembers his math teacher. Of her he says, "On the outside was a tough teacher, but inside was a very nice person." On trips the class took with her, her students discovered she was a consummate "laugher." She enjoyed what she did both in and out of the classroom, and because of her enthusiasm for life—including for her subject specialty—her students learned to release their previous dread of studying math. Kevin recalls that "if you had a question, she would stop and explain how to reach a solution. And no matter how long the problem took, she always remained cheerful." Kevin is now studying to be a math teacher.

Lois's third grade teacher was particularly special to her, for a very good reason. "One time," as Lois tells the story, "we made gingerbread men out of real dough and baked them and then decorated them. While we were doing ours, my teacher made two to give to her grandchildren. After school, my friend and I had just started on our way home when we dropped our sack, breaking both our gingerbread men. We went back to school in tears—our teacher was still there—and without hesitation she gave us the two she had made for her grandchildren. She could have hugged us and sent us home with our broken cookies, but she didn't. She hugged us, and even though she'd had special plans for them, sent us home with two intact cookies."

But sometimes, like Sheri, we don't know what it is about a teacher that makes him or her memorable. "The teacher I admire most," says Sheri, "is my high school home economics teacher, but I don't know why. I just remember her the best. It's really hard to figure out why she was so good with us. She was probably in her late fifties, maybe even into her sixties, and in those days we normally rejected anyone we suspected of being 'old-fashioned,' you know what I mean?" Sheri just shakes her head. "But I loved her. . . . Most of all, I guess, was that she was caring and flexible. She would let me come in and sew whenever I wanted. It was relaxing to be there, even sort of comforting. I guess more than the sewing itself, that was what I liked. Just being in her comforting presence."

Gary recalls Joe, his high school sociology teacher who was also his football coach. As Gary tells it, "Joe wasn't 'moody,' he was consistent. The best thing Joe did for me was help me grow up." At one point during his senior year, an event happened which Gary still is reluctant to be specific about. Nevertheless, it severely depressed him, leaving him in almost suicidal despair. His parents recognized that something was terribly wrong with Gary, though they did not know what. What they did know was that their son looked up to Joe, and so they went to see him, asking him to try to help Gary. Joe willingly and gladly did.

Today, Gary says, because of his parents' "interference" and Joe's intercession, he is alive and eager to become a teacher, and hopefully someday, a parent as well.

In one of his many inimitable essays published in *A Few Minutes with Andy Rooney,* Mr. Rooney treats us to a look at his serious side:

> The only description of Christ ever found purporting to have been written by a contemporary is not generally accepted as authentic, but it has been the basis of many great works of art. It was said to have been written by a public official in Jerusalem during Christ's lifetime. "There has appeared here in our time a man of great power named Jesus Christ. The people call him a prophet of truth, and his disciples the Son of God. He raises the dead and cures the sick. He is in stature a man of middle height and well-proportioned. He has a venerable face. His hair is the color of ripe chestnuts—smooth almost to the ears, but above them waving and curling, with a slight bluish radiancy, and it flows over his shoulders. It is parted in the middle on the top of his head after the fashion of the people of Nazareth. His brow is smooth and very calm, with a face without a wrinkle or a blemish, lightly tinged with red. His nose and mouth are faultless. His beard is luxuriant and uncreased, of the same color as his hair—not long, but parted at the chin. His countenance is full of simplicity and love. His eyes are expressive and brilliant. He is terrible in reproof, sweet and gentle in admonition, cheerful without ceasing to be grave. His figure is slender and erect. His hands and arms are beautiful to see. He is the fairest of the children of God."[5]

Because of the absence of photography and paintings, we cannot be sure of Christ's actual countenance. We cannot duplicate his physical being with any accuracy—which, of course, is of no real consequence to what we *can* do. We can distill his essence, drop by drop. Through reliance on him, and through cultivating our human natures to more nearly represent his, we can help to depict the multitudinous faces of Christ to a world of students who are in desperate need of seeing them.

But I'm Not a Teacher: Where Do I Go from Here?

In *Inviting School Success,* Purkey and Novak include helpful
lists of specific techniques for nonteaching personnel entitled
"What School Bus Drivers Can Do," "What School Secre-
taries Can Do," and so forth—the point being, you don't have
to be a teacher in a classroom to have an impact on students.
Offering invitations to parents and other community leaders
outside the school to become involved in students' lives is just as
important as is offering invitations to non-certificated personnel
within schools. Indeed, it is a crucial, frequently overlooked
part of an educator's responsibility. But if invitations for involvement are not forthcoming, parents and other community
leaders must not be reluctant to invite themselves.

Specific suggestions do help, of course, and we will get to
some, but theologian and teacher Richard Foster provides a
wise caution. He reminds us that there is an extremely important framework by which we need to evaluate any roles we
choose to play. Through this framework, our attitudes about
service must be screened. In *Celebration of Discipline,* Dr. Foster proposes that we give up the urge to seek something specific
to do, and instead, open our lives to true servanthood—a very
different and far more Christlike approach.

> Right here we must see the difference between choosing to serve
> and choosing to be a servant. When we choose to serve we are still
> in charge. We decide whom we will serve and when we will
> serve. . . . But when we choose to be a servant we give up the right
> to be in charge. There is a great freedom in this. If we voluntarily
> choose to be taken advantage of, then we cannot be manipulated.
> When we choose to be a servant we surrender the right to decide
> who and when we will serve. We become available and vulner-
> able.[6]

I challenge all of us, both teachers and nonteachers, to find
ways to be "servants" to schools and, more directly, to students

themselves. We must make ourselves available. We must open ourselves, or "unprotect" ourselves—which is to say, we must allow for the possibility of being exposed to critical need and, whether we feel "up" to the task or not, of helping meet that need. Because you have read this book, you are by that very act indicating your interest in seeing schools achieve excellence. You and I can both trust that you truly want to find ways to divert the "rising tide of mediocrity." It is obvious you care about kids and their education, or you would never have made it this far in our study.

While I intend to point out some specific ways of getting involved in educational organizations, I urge you to bear in mind that none of these are "do-all" or "end-all" suggestions. Additional activities just as worthy of your consideration are limited only by the amount of availability and vulnerability you yourself commit to. Keep knocking on doors until you are al- lowed into children's lives. It is not they who are keeping you out. As a beginning place only, the following suggestions are offered.

"Helping-hand" activities solidify bonds between the school and the community. Through partnerships with businesses, teachers and students see unavailable services become available. One example of this is managers and clerical staff in, say, a retail store all pitching together to read textbook assignments onto cassette tapes. For both elementary and secondary students with reading problems, such audio help is invaluable. These students are freed to learn material that would otherwise elude them.

Another service businesses adopting schools sometimes in- stitute in an elementary school is that of providing adults who willingly spend their lunch hour on the school playground. Montaigne's observation that "children at play are not playing about; their games should be seen as their most serious-minded activity" is understood very well by these community volun- teers. Caring people—and businesses that adopt schools are peopled with such employees—are glad for the opportunity to serve in both supervisory and role modeling capacities during moments of children's "most serious-minded activity."

A business vulnerable to the needs of teens often commits a certain number of part-time jobs to those who attend the "adopted school." And in those businesses that adopt high schools or junior highs, as well as elementary schools, after-school tutoring can be provided. Under this arrangement, young people are invited to stop by the store or firm on their way home from school for help with homework or for specialized tutoring. A willing adult assumes administrative responsibility for meeting the needs of these "drop-ins." It is also a good opportunity for so-called "latch-key" children to receive supervision and adult guidance, instead of having nowhere to go but an empty house.

A second successful program implemented by volunteers in many schools is what is generally known as the "Foster Grandparent Program." Because of our increasingly mobile society, most children today do not live near paternal or maternal grandparents. Consequently, contact with senior citizens is kept at a minimum. Yet this is one of the most crucial cross-generational bondings there is. Older adults, experienced in years and in life, are mellowing influences on children. Contact with them is very different from that with career-minded parents or with those of parental age, who are more driven and distracted by the workaday world than are those already retired from it. Indeed, bringing children and senior citizens together is important for another reason, too: children can fill a void in a lonely grandparent's life.

One school I know has a foster grandparent assigned to every room in the building. A schedule is worked out each week between the "grandparent" and the teacher, determining when the grandparent will be available to come to school and when such visits will best fit into the teacher's plans. The grandparent—either a grandmother or a grandfather, it is not impor-

tant which, though actually one of each would be ideal—
provides an extra pair of eyes and ears and a set of able hands.
Busy teachers welcome such help.

Perhaps on one day the grandparent will tutor a child or a
small group of children experiencing difficulty with a certain
math concept. Perhaps on another day the teacher will set time
aside for the grandparent to talk with the whole class about
what was different when he or she went to grade school and
studied, say, math or science. Perhaps the grandparent will eat
lunch at a table with the children, doing nothing more than
simply sharing in informal, friendly chatter. Or the grandparent
may come to the classroom to teach the particulars of his or her
hobby—maybe, for instance, each child will add a square to a
quilt the grandparent is making. This program has wonderful
possibilities for any community that is open to being open.

In another burst of enthusiasm for sharing responsibilities
with the neighborhood school, one group of innovative, nonteaching adults decided, with the principal's grateful endorsement, to set up an "outdoor classroom" for students. A small
plot of ground was made available to them, and these caring
adults (some of them college students, many of them parents)
came on weekends and during the early evenings—in partnership with whichever children and teachers were available at
those times—to plant specimens of almost every tree, bush, and
flower native to their state. The enterprising adults provided
the specimens and most of the labor. The school itself agreed to
undertake the upkeep. Each class in the building was assigned
its own section of landscaped ground for watering, weeding,
and the like. Now, several years after it first began, the outdoor
classroom is lush and green and not only provides a living lesson
in botany, it also provides a readily available respite for such
important activities as reading a story under a shady tree after
lunch. Indeed, in its many uses, it has become a beloved addition
to the total school complex.

Unfortunately, a fourth idea for school and community part-

nership—the parent-teacher organization—has all but disappeared in many places. Those PTAs and PTOs that have stayed
alive have done so through commitment to particular ideals,
such as focusing their energies on one well-chosen, worthwhile
project annually. A project currently receiving careful parental
attention is RIF ("Reading is FUN-damental"). RIF began as a
federally funded program to promote recreational reading. As
did many educational programs whose origin was federal
monies, RIF lost its initial funding.

The idea of the RIF program is to provide a free, self-selected
book to every child in the country every year. Boxes and boxes
of quality paperback books are shipped to schools from various
book services, such as Scholastic Books. Throughout each
school building, every child is brought to a main "library" (it
might be the gymnasium or another room large enough to hold
long tables loaded with a smorgasbord of free books). Each child
is then given the opportunity to pick out and take home "for
keeps" any book of his or her choice. It is one of the most terrific
incentives to read for fun and recreation ever devised. Anyone
who has watched a RIF Day in the making knows that it is a
special, treasured occasion in a child's school life.

And it still continues to be so in many schools. When the
federal funds dried up, parents in several districts got together
and elected to resuscitate RIF. The funds for RIF now come
locally, from chili feeds and fun nights and creative money-
making ventures. Committed community folks are often kids'
best friends.

In addition, nonteaching personnel—such as parents and
other community adults—can build bookshelves and reading
lofts and sturdy playground equipment for schools suffering
from limited funds. Nonteaching personnel can become volun-
teer storytellers, behaving (as I have personally witnessed)
rather like the wandering troubadours and minstrels of old as
they travel in costume from classroom to classroom, carrying
with them the delight of oral language. They can provide talent
and technical assistance on a whole array of specialized art

projects (most elementary schools no longer have access to the services of a professional art instructor). In fact, they can donate the knowledge gleaned from their hobbies and interests through all types of adjunct teaching opportunities.

Responsible adults who care about children can help in other, less classroom-oriented ways, too. Some parents are already working in tandem with the schools to provide strategic homes along walking routes as "block" houses, even visibly sign-posting them that way. Letting children in your neighborhood know you are available to them, should they need you, is a valuable contribution to young people's lives, especially as more mothers work and more children are alone after school. However, the sign alone will not make the contribution. Only a deliberate effort to get to know each other as friends and as neighbors will allow children to feel comfortable enough to make use of the block parent when a trusted adult is needed.

Again I challenge all of us—myself included—to discover our own individual ways of making these and other things happen. Apathetic people, or people only half-heartedly interested in functioning as servants to schools, do not help eliminate mediocrity. They breed it. Such people do not contribute to excellence in children's education or in anyone's education, including their own. Excellence cannot subsist on less than total commitment to stemming mediocrity's tide.

And Christians, in particular, have no excuse for biding their time and waiting on others to do these things first. Christians must be at the forefront of exemplifying servanthood. Judgment against others who fail to serve is not our right. Through Christ, it is *we* who have been commissioned to serve. " 'The Christian ideal,' it is said, 'has not been tried and found wanting,' " G. K. Chesterton reminds us, " 'it has been found difficult and left untried.' "7

Schools have need for authentic servants. They do not have need for more adult involvement of the kind novelist John Updike writes about in *Rabbit, Run*. Bewildered himself, Updike's adult in turn bewilders children. Yet, through mindlessness or

limited understanding, or just through passively following historical precedent, we put ourselves in danger of being this
person.

> You climb up through the little grades and then get to the top and
> everybody cheers; with the sweat in your eyebrows you can't see
> very well and the noise swirls around you and lifts you up, and then
> you're out, not forgotten at first, just out, and it feels good and cool
> and free. You're out, and sort of melt, and keep lifting, until you
> become like to these kids just one more piece of the sky of adults that
> hangs over them in the town, a piece that for some queer reason has
> clouded and visited them.[8]

Let us not become just "one more piece of the sky of adults"
hanging over children. Let us, shunning the conventionality of
Updike's "clouded" vision, stand firm in the clarity of our own.
And let us realize that our vision receives its clarity from the life
of Jesus Christ. Within his life is a glorious plan for the salvation of children's emotional and intellectual health, a plan for
nurturing and achievement and growth. Within Christ's life
is a plan for *excellence*.

Because the kind of teaching required to attain this excellence
is detached from witnessing and preaching, it fits every school
and every classroom. Public and private and parochial schools
are equally served by Christ's plan. Yet, by attending to the
requirements for intellectual and emotional growth, relevant as
they are by themselves, we sow seeds for spiritual insights. It is
called "paving the way."

As Christ demonstrates, to teach Christianly you must understand the importance of modeling and loving. You must
know about the importance of healing and enabling. And, over
the strong foundation of these four qualities, to teach Christianly you must prod. With modeling and loving, with healing
and enabling as its base, prodding can risk being firm enough to
push growth in areas students would not otherwise explore.

Our new road to "salvation"—a way all Christian teachers

can travel, including those in public schools—is really an old road, looked at anew. We must fine-tune children's minds so that they will know and understand the significance of truth and beauty to their lives, so that they will become lifelong seekers after it. Important as other skills are, this is the most basic learning there is for each of us—developing our innate aesthetic sense, our ability to appreciate and experience loveliness in all its many forms. Indeed, it is that capability which sets us apart from other earthly creatures. And it is that capability which ultimately enables us to understand the love and goodness of God.

Our ceaseless worrying about education has not enacted change. What shall we do, we ask? We are what we should "do." Children's education never ends, and neither does ours. That fact embodies one very good reason why it is never too late to become involved.

Through education's enduring essentiality—which is to say, through the lifelong nature of learning—each child's teacher must be seen as more than someone with a degree from a college or university, more than someone who holds a legally signed and sealed teaching certificate. Each child's teacher is, by Christian definition, all of us.

NOTES

Introduction

1. National Commission on Excellence in Education, *A Nation at Risk: The Imperative for Educational Reform* (Washington, D.C.: U.S. Government Printing Office, 1983), p. 23.

2. Jonathan Kozol, *Death at an Early Age* (New York: Bantam Books, 1967), pp. 1–2.

Chapter 1

1. Nat Hentoff, *Our Children Are Dying* (New York: Viking Press, 1966), p. 8.

2. David L. McKenna, *The Jesus Model* (Waco, TX: Word Books, 1977), p. 59.

3. Ibid., p. 53.

4. Anne Morrow Lindbergh, *Gift from the Sea* (New York: Vintage Books, 1955), p. 42.

5. Abraham Maslow, *Toward a Psychology of Being* (Princeton, NJ: Van Nostrand, 1968).

6. Raymond L. Cramer, *The Psychology of Jesus and Mental Health* (Grand Rapids, MI: Zondervan, 1978), p. 157.

Chapter 2

1. "Bringing up Superbaby," *Newsweek,* March 28, 1983, pp. 62–68.

2. Richard J. Foster, *Celebration of Discipline: The Path to Spiritual Growth* (San Francisco: Harper & Row, 1978), p. 1.

3. "Bringing up Superbaby," *Newsweek,* p. 68.

4. Reinhold Niebuhr, *Faith and History: A Comparison of Christian and Modern Views of History* (New York: Charles Scribner's, 1949), p. 197.

5. Suzanne Clauser, *A Girl Named Sooner* (New York: Avon, 1972), p. 75.

6. C. S. Lewis, *The Four Loves* (New York: Harcourt Brace Jovanovich, 1960), p. 20.

7. Harper Lee, *To Kill a Mockingbird* (Philadelphia: J. B. Lippincott, 1960), p. 36.

8. Ernest Boyer, "Reflections on the Great Debate of '83," *Phi Delta Kappan* (April 1984), p. 525.

Chapter 3

1. Benjamin Bloom, *Human Characteristics and School Learning* (New York: McGraw-Hill, 1976).

2. David Elkind, *The Hurried Child: Growing Up Too Fast Too Soon* (Reading, MS: Addison-Wesley, 1981), p. xii.

3. Geoffrey Cowan, *See No Evil* (New York: Touchstone, 1980).

4. Daniel Fader, *The Naked Children* (New York: Macmillan, 1971), p. 35.

5. Megan Marshall, "Musical Wonder Kids," *Boston Globe Magazine*, July 25, 1981.

6. Paul R. Ackerman and Murray M. Kappelman, *Signals: What Your Child Is Really Telling You* (New York: Dial Press, 1978).

7. Agnes Sanford, *The Healing Light* (Plainfield, NJ: Logos, 1972), p. 114.

8. William L. Vaswig, *I Prayed, He Answered* (Minneapolis: Augsburg, 1977), p. 80.

9. Sanford, *The Healing Light*, pp. 157–58.

10. Ibid., p. 53.

11. Marie Winn, *Children without Childhood: Growing Up Too Fast in the World of Sex and Drugs* (New York: Penguin Books, 1983), pp. 3–7.

12. Ibid., p. 209.

13. Russell Baker, *Growing Up* (New York: Congdon & Weed, 1982), p. 42.

14. Cramer, *The Psychology of Jesus*, pp. 173–74.

15. Ibid., p. 182.

16. Abraham Maslow, *Motivation and Personality*, 2d. ed. (New York: Harper & Row, 1970), p. 254.

Chapter 4

1. Daniel Selakovich, *Schooling in America* (New York: Longman, 1984), p. 36.
2. Alice Virginia Keliher, *Talks with Teachers*, foreword by Eleanor Roosevelt (Darien, CT: Educational Pub. Corp., 1958).
3. Colin Greer, *The Great School Legend* (New York: Basic Books, 1972), p. 152.
4. Richard Hofstadter, *Anti-Intellectualism in American Life* (New York: Vintage Books, 1966), p. 305.
5. William Watson Purkey and John M. Novak, *Inviting School Success: A Self-Concept Approach to Teaching and Learning*, 2d. ed. (Belmont, CA: Wadsworth, 1984), p. 2.
6. Guy Lefrancois, *Psychology for Teaching: A Bear Rarely Faces the Front*, 4th ed. (Belmont, CA: Wadsworth, 1982), p. 151.
7. B. F. Skinner, *The Technology of Teaching* (New York: Appleton-Century-Crofts, 1968), pp. 5–12.
8. Harry Dawe, "Teaching: A Performing Art," *Phi Delta Kappan*, April 1984, p. 548.
9. Carl R. Rogers, *Freedom to Learn* (Columbus, OH: Charles E. Merrill, 1969); Carl R. Rogers, *A Way of Being* (Boston: Houghton Mifflin, 1980).
10. Lefrancois, *Psychology for Teaching*, p. 188.
11. Ibid., p. 194.
12. Lewis, *The Four Loves*, p. 163.

Chapter 5

Donald Kraybill, *The Upside-Down Kingdom* (Scottdale, PA: Herald Press, 1978), p. 29.
2. James Herndon, *How to Survive in Your Native Land* (New York: Simon and Schuster, 1971), p. 116.
3. Maria Montessori, *The Montessori Method*, trans. by Anne E. George (New York: Schocken Books, 1964), p. 220.
4. W. Lambert Gardiner, *The Psychology of Teaching* (Monterey, CA: Brooks/Cole, 1980), p. 145.

5. Neil Postman and Charles Weingartner, *Teaching as a Subversive Activity* (New York: Dell, 1969), p. 61.

6. Robert B. Sund and Arthur Carin, *Creative Questioning and Sensitive Listening Techniques: A Self-Concept Approach* (Columbus, OH: Charles E. Merrill, 1978).

7. Elkind, *The Hurried Child,* p. 170.

8. R. L. Veniga and J. P. Spradley, *The Work Stress Connection* (Boston: Little, Brown, 1981).

9. Winn, *Children without Childhood,* p. 81.

10. Lilian G. Katz, "What Is Basic for Young Children?" in Glen Hass, ed., *Curriculum Planning: A New Approach,* 3rd ed., (Boston: Allyn and Bacon, 1980), pp. 275–78.

11. Tom Sine, *The Mustard Seed Conspiracy: You Can Make a Difference in Tomorrow's Troubled World* (Waco, TX: Word Books, 1981), p. 236.

12. John W. Gardner, *Excellence: Can We Be Equal and Excellent Too?* (New York: Harper Bros., 1961), p. 86.

13. G. K. Chesterton, "A Fragment" from *The Coloured Lands,* in W. Lambert Gardiner, *The Psychology of Teaching* (Monterey, CA: Brooks/Cole, 1980), p. 196.

Chapter 6

1. Alexander Solzhenitsyn, "The Exhausted West," Commencement Address at Harvard University, June 8, 1978.

2. Martin Luther King, Jr., Speech at Civil Rights March on Washington, August 28, 1963.

3. John Dewey, "What Psychology Can Do for the Teacher," in Reginald Archambault, ed., *John Dewey on Education: Selected Writings* (New York: Random House, 1964).

4. Constance Kamii, "Autonomy: The Aim of Education Envisioned by Piaget," *Phi Delta Kappan,* February 1984, p. 410.

5. Lawrence Kohlberg, "Stages of Moral Development as a Basis for Moral Education," in C. Beck, E. V. Sullivan, & B. Crittendon, eds., *Moral Education: Interdisciplinary Approaches* (Toronto: University of Toronto Press, 1971); Lawrence Kohlberg, "Moral Stages and Moralization," in T. Likona, ed., *Moral Development: Current Theory and Research* (New York: Holt, Rinehart & Winston, 1976); Lawrence Kohlberg, "The Cognitive-Developmental Approach to

Moral Education," in G. Hass, ed., *Curriculum Planning: A New Approach*, 3d ed. (Boston: Allyn & Bacon, 1980).

6. G. K. Chesterton, *A Defense of Nonsense* in John Bartlett, ed., *Bartlett's Familiar Quotations*, 15th ed., (Boston: Little, Brown, 1980), p. 742.

7. Robert D. Strom and Harold W. Bernard, *Educational Psychology* (Monterey, CA: Brooks/Cole, 1982), p. 135.

8. Alvin Toffler, *Future Shock* (New York: Bantam Books, 1970), p. 417.

9. Glen Heathers, "Education to Meet the Psychological Requirements for Living in the Future," *Journal of Teacher Education* 25, no. 2 (Summer 1974), pp. 108–112.

10. Urie Bronfenbrenner, *Two Worlds of Childhood: U.S. and U.S.S.R.* (New York: Simon and Schuster, 1972).

11. James R. Baker and Arthur B. Siegler, Jr., eds., *Lord of the Flies: Text, Notes, and Criticism* (New York: Putnam, 1964).

12. Bruno Bettelheim, *The Uses of Enchantment: The Meaning and Importance of Fairy Tales* (New York: Vintage, 1977), p. 5.

13. William W. Wayson and Thomas J. Lasley, "Climates for Excellence: Schools That Foster Self-Discipline," *Phi Delta Kappan*, February 1984, p. 419.

14. William Glasser, *Schools without Failure* (New York: Harper & Row, 1969), p. 7.

15. Elkind, *The Hurried Child*, p. 30.

16. John Underwood, "A Game Plan for America," *Sports Illustrated*, February 23, 1981, p. 66.

17. Mortimer J. Adler, *The Paideia Proposal: An Educational Manifesto* (New York: Macmillan, 1982).

18. Mortimer J. Adler, "The Reform of Public Schools," *The Center Magazine*, September/October 1983, p. 13.

19. *A Nation at Risk*, pp. 34–35.

20. Ibid., p. 7.

21. Joseph F. Callahan and Leonard H. Clark, *Introduction to American Education: Planning for Competence*, 2d. ed. (New York: Macmillan, 1983), pp. 320–21.

22. Foster, *Celebration of Discipline*, p. 8.

23. Marilyn O. Karmel and Louis J. Karmel, *Growing and Becoming: Development from Conception through Adolescence* (New York: Macmillan, 1984), p. 414.

24. Ibid.
25. "Climates for Excellence," *Phi Delta Kappan,* pp. 419–420.

Chapter 7

1. Louis Fischer, *The Life of Mahatma Gandhi* (New York: Harper & Row, 1950).
2. D. Elton Trueblood, *Abraham Lincoln: Theologian of American Anguish* (New York: Harper & Row, 1973).
3. Anne Frank, *Anne Frank: Diary of a Young Girl* (New York: Random House, 1956), excerpted from the entry for July 15, 1944.
4. Milton Mayeroff, *On Caring* (New York: Harper & Row, 1971), p. 13.
5. Jerry Cook and Stanley C. Baldwin, *Love, Acceptance & Forgiveness: Equipping the Church to Be Truly Christian in a Non-Christian World* (Ventura, CA: Regal Books, 1979), p. 121.
6. Douglas Simpson and Michael J. B. Jackson, *The Teacher as Philosopher: A Primer in Philosophy of Education* (Toronto: Methuen, 1984), p. 3.
7. Ibid., p. 12.
8. Archibald D. Hart, *Coping with Depression in the Ministry and Other Helping Professions* (Waco, TX: Word Books, 1984), p. 113.
9. Dewey J. Carducci and Judith B. Carducci, *The Caring Classroom: A Guide for Teachers Troubled by the Difficult Student and Classroom Disruption* (Palo Alto, CA: Bull, 1984), p. 206.
10. Hans Küng, *On Being a Christian,* trans. by Edward Quinn (Garden City: Doubleday, 1976), p. 530.
11. Herbert Kohl, *Insight: The Substance and Rewards of Teaching* (Menlo Park, CA: Addison-Wesley, 1982), p. 226.
12. Ibid., p. 170.
13. Hart, *Coping with Depression,* pp. 97–98.
14. Peter Ustinov, *Dear Me* (Boston: Little, Brown, 1977), p. 238.

Chapter 8

1. Paul Aurandt, *Paul Harvey's the Rest of the Story,* Lynne Harvey, ed. (New York: Bantam Books, 1977), p. 47.
2. Kevin Ryan, Suzanne Burkholder, and Debra Hallock Phillips, *The Workbook: Exploring Careers in Teaching* (Columbus, OH: Charles E. Merrill, 1983), p. 161.

3. Natalie Babbitt, *Tuck Everlasting* (New York: Farrar, Strauss & Giroux, 1975), p. 57.

4. Andrew A. Rooney, *A Few Minutes with Andy Rooney* (New York: Atheneum, 1981), p. 245.

5. Ibid., p. 244.

6. Foster, *Celebration of Discipline,* p. 115.

7. G. K. Chesterton, *What's Wrong with the World* in John Bartlett, ed., *Bartlett's Familiar Quotations,* 15th ed. (Boston: Little, Brown, 1980), p. 742.

8. John Updike, *Rabbit, Run* (New York: Knopf, 1960), p. 5.

RECOMMENDED READINGS
FOR FURTHER INSIGHTS

Ackerman, Paul R. and Kappelman, Murray M. *Signals: What Your Child Is Really Telling You*. New York: Dial Press, 1978.

Adler, Mortimer J. *The Paideia Proposal: An Educational Manifesto*. New York: Macmillan, 1982.

Armstrong, Michael. *Closely Observed Children: The Diary of a Primary Classroom*. London, England: Writers and Readers, in association with Chameleon, 1980.

Barnette, Helen P. *Your Child's Mind: Making the Most of Public Schools*. Philadelphia: Westminster Press, 1984.

Bloom, Benjamin. *All Our Children Learning: A Primer for Parents, Teachers, and Other Educators*. New York: McGraw-Hill, 1981.

_____, ed. *Developing Talent in Young People*. New York: Ballantine, 1984.

Bronfenbrenner, Urie. *Two Worlds of Childhood: U.S. and U.S.S.R.* New York: Simon and Schuster, 1972.

Carducci, Dewey J. and Carducci, Judith B. *The Caring Classroom: A Guide for Teachers Troubled by the Difficult Student and Classroom Disruption*. Palo Alto, CA: Bull, 1984.

Clapp, Rodney. "Vanishing Childhood." *Christianity Today*, pt. 1 (May 18, 1984):12–19; pt. 2 (June 15, 1984):18–24.

Cook, Jerry and Baldwin, Stanley C. *Love, Acceptance, and Forgiveness: Equipping the Church to Be Truly Christian in a Non-Christian World*. Ventura, CA: Regal Books, 1979.

Elkind, David. *The Hurried Child: Growing Up Too Fast Too Soon*. Menlo Park, CA: Addison-Wesley, 1981.

Everhart, Robert B., ed. *The Public School Monopoly: A Critical Analysis of Education and the State in American Society*. Cambridge, MS: Ballinger/Harper & Row, 1982.

Fader, Daniel. *The Naked Children*. New York: Macmillan, 1971.

Ferreiro, Emilia and Teberosky, Ana. *Literacy Before Schooling*.

Translated by Karen Goodman Castro. Preface by Yetta Goodman. Exeter, NH: Heinemann, 1982.

Gardner, John W. *Excellence*. Rev. ed. New York: Norton, 1984.

Glasser, William. *Schools without Failure*. New York: Harper & Row, 1969.

Hainstock, Elizabeth G. *Teaching Montessori in the Home: The Pre-school Years*. New York: New American Library, 1976.

Holt, John. *Instead of Education: Ways to Help People Do Things Better*. New York: Dell, 1976.

Hunt, Gladys. *Honey for a Child's Heart: The Imaginative Use of Books in Family Life*. Grand Rapids, MI: Zondervan, 1978.

Kohl, Herbert. *Insight: The Substance and Rewards of Teaching*. Menlo Park, CA: Addison-Wesley, 1982.

———. *Basic Skills: A Plan for Your Child, a Program for All Children*. New York: Bantam Books, 1984.

Kramer, Rita. *In Defense of the Family: Raising Children in America Today*. New York: Basic Books, 1983.

Mayeroff, Milton. *On Caring*. New York: Harper & Row, 1971.

National Commission on Excellence in Education. *A Nation at Risk: The Imperative for Educational Reform*. Washington, D.C.: U.S. Government Printing Office, 1983.

Packard, Vance. *Our Endangered Children: Growing Up in a Changing World*. Boston: Little, Brown, 1983.

Postman, Neil. *The Disappearance of Childhood*. New York: Dell, 1982.

Postman, Neil and Weingartner, Charles. *Teaching as a Subversive Activity*. New York: Dell, 1969.

Purkey, William Watson and Novak, John M. *Inviting School Success: A Self-Concept Approach to Teaching and Learning*. 2d ed. Belmont, CA: Wadsworth, 1984.

Rogers, Carl R. *A Way of Being*. Boston: Houghton Mifflin, 1980.

Sanford, Agnes. *The Healing Light*. Plainfield, NJ: Logos, 1972.

Schimmels, Cliff. *How to Help Your Child Survive and Thrive in the Public School*. Old Tappan, NJ: Revell, 1982.

Sine, Tom. *The Mustard Seed Conspiracy: You Can Make a Difference in Tomorrow's Troubled World*. Waco, TX: Word Books, 1981.

Strom, Robert D., ed. *Growing through Play: Readings for Parents and Teachers*. Monterey, CA: Brooks/Cole, 1982.

Taylor, Denny. *Family Literacy: Young Children Learning to Read and Write*. Exeter, NH: Heinemann, 1983.

Trelease, Jim. *The Read-Aloud Handbook*. New York: Penguin Books, 1982.
Van Alstine, George. *The Christian and the Public Schools*. Nashville, TN: Abingdon, 1982.
Winn, Marie. *Children without Childhood: Growing Up Too Fast in the World of Sex and Drugs*. New York: Penguin Books, 1983.